Daily

Paragraph
Editing

GRADE 8

Writing: Emily Hutchinson
Content Editing: Robin Kelly
Lisa Vitarisi Mathews
Teera Safi
Copy Editing: Anna Pelligra
Art Direction: Cheryl Puckett
Art Resources: Kathy Kopp
Cover Design: Cheryl Puckett
Design/Production: Carolina Caird
Susan Lovell

EMC 2838

Evan-Moor®
Helping Children Learn

Visit
teaching-standards.com
to view a correlation
of this book.
This is a free service.

*Correlated to State and
Common Core State Standards*

**Congratulations on your purchase of some of the
finest teaching materials in the world.**

For information about other Evan-Moor products, call 1-800-777-4362,
fax 1-800-777-4332, or visit our Web site, www.evan-moor.com.
Entire contents © 2013 EVAN-MOOR CORP.
18 Lower Ragsdale Drive, Monterey, CA 93940-5746. Printed in USA.

CPSIA: Printed by McNaughton & Gunn, Saline, MI USA.[5/2015]

Contents

Introduction

Why Daily Paragraph Editing?

This book is designed to help students master and retain grade-level skills in language mechanics and expression through focused, daily practice. The passages represent the writing forms that students encounter in their daily reading and writing activities across the curriculum. A weekly writing activity allows students to apply the skills they have been practicing throughout the week.

What's in This Book?

Daily Paragraph Editing contains lessons for 36 weeks, with a separate lesson for each day. Each week's lessons for Monday through Thursday consist of individual reproducible paragraphs that contain errors in the following skills:

- capitalization
- language usage
- punctuation
- spelling, and more

Each Friday lesson consists of a writing prompt that directs students to write in response to the week's composition. This gives students the opportunity to apply the skills they have practiced during the week in their own writing. Students gain experience writing in a variety of forms, with the support of familiar models.

How Does It Work?

Students correct the errors in each daily portion of the composition by marking directly on the page. A reproducible sheet of Proofreading Marks (see page 168) helps familiarize students with the standard form for marking corrections on written text. Full-page Editing Keys show corrections for all errors. Error Summaries help teachers identify the targeted skills in each week's lessons so teachers can plan to review or introduce the specific skills needed by their students.

A reproducible Language Handbook (pages 169–176) outlines the usage and mechanics rules for students to follow as they edit. The Handbook includes examples to help familiarize students with how the conventions of language and mechanics are applied in authentic writing.

When corrected and read together, the paragraphs that make up the week's lesson form a cohesive composition that also serves as a writing model for students. The compositions cover a broad range of expository and narrative writing forms from across the curriculum, including the following:

- nonfiction texts on grade-level topics in science and social studies
- biographies, book reviews, persuasive essays, journal entries, and letters
- myths, fables, historical fiction, personal narratives, and realistic fiction

Student's daily lesson pages for Monday through Thursday

Indicates the writing form modeled in the weekly lesson

Identifies the day and week

Provides text with errors for students to correct

Alerts students to skills that may be more challenging

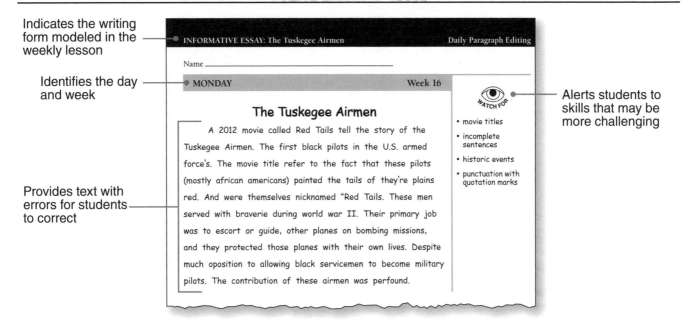

INFORMATIVE ESSAY: The Tuskegee Airmen — Daily Paragraph Editing

Name _____

MONDAY — Week 16

The Tuskegee Airmen

A 2012 movie called Red Tails tell the story of the Tuskegee Airmen. The first black pilots in the U.S. armed force's. The movie title refer to the fact that these pilots (mostly african americans) painted the tails of they're plains red. And were themselves nicknamed "Red Tails. These men served with braverie during world war II. Their primary job was to escort or guide, other planes on bombing missions, and they protected those planes with their own lives. Despite much oposition to allowing black servicemen to become military pilots. The contribution of these airmen was perfound.

WATCH FOR
- movie titles
- incomplete sentences
- historic events
- punctuation with quotation marks

Friday writing prompts

Identifies the week

Prompts students to write a composition in the same form as the weekly lesson

Provides sample lead sentences to support reluctant writers

Indicates the writing form and the title of the weekly lesson

Provides hints to help students address skills specific to the writing form

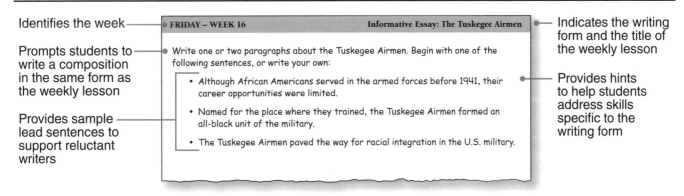

FRIDAY – WEEK 16 — Informative Essay: The Tuskegee Airmen

Write one or two paragraphs about the Tuskegee Airmen. Begin with one of the following sentences, or write your own:

- Although African Americans served in the armed forces before 1941, their career opportunities were limited.
- Named for the place where they trained, the Tuskegee Airmen formed an all-black unit of the military.
- The Tuskegee Airmen paved the way for racial integration in the U.S. military.

Teacher's full-sized annotated Editing Key

Indicates the writing form modeled in the weekly lesson

Identifies the day and week

Shows the student text with corrections marked in red. (See page 168 for Proofreading Marks resource page.)

Indicates the writing form

Summarizes the errors in the day's lesson by category

(Some students may be more successful if you share the Error Summary with them before they read and edit the paragraph.)

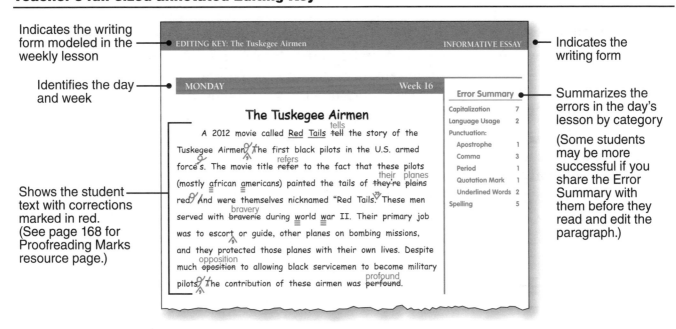

EDITING KEY: The Tuskegee Airmen — INFORMATIVE ESSAY

MONDAY — Week 16

The Tuskegee Airmen

tells
A 2012 movie called <u>Red Tails</u> ~~tell~~ the story of the
Tuskegee Airmen. The first black pilots in the U.S. armed
refers
force's. The movie title ~~refer~~ to the fact that these pilots
their planes
(mostly <u>african</u> <u>americans</u>) painted the tails of ~~they're plains~~
red. And were themselves nicknamed "Red Tails." These men
bravery
served with ~~braverie~~ during <u>world war</u> II. Their primary job
was to escort, or guide, other planes on bombing missions,
and they protected those planes with their own lives. Despite
opposition
much ~~oposition~~ to allowing black servicemen to become military
profound
pilots. The contribution of these airmen was ~~perfound~~.

Error Summary

Capitalization	7
Language Usage	2
Punctuation:	
Apostrophe	1
Comma	3
Period	1
Quotation Mark	1
Underlined Words	2
Spelling	5

How to Use *Daily Paragraph Editing*

You can use *Daily Paragraph Editing* with the whole class or assign lessons for individual practice. Presentation strategies are outlined below. Find the approach that works best for you and your students. It's a good idea, though, to reproduce and distribute all four daily lessons for a given week on Monday. That way, students can use the previous day's lesson for reference as the week progresses.

Directed Group Lessons

The *Daily Paragraph Editing* lessons will be most successful if you introduce each one as a group activity. Have students mark up their copies as you work through the lesson together. Continue presenting the Monday through Thursday lessons to the entire class until you are confident that students are familiar with the editing process. Try one of the following methods to direct group lessons:

Option 1

Display the day's editing lesson using a projection system. Read the text aloud just as it is written, including all of the errors. Read it a second time, using phrasing and intonation that would be appropriate if all punctuation were correct. Guide students in correcting errors; mark the corrections on the displayed page. Encourage students to discuss the reason for each correction; explain or clarify any rules that are unfamiliar.

Option 2

Display the day's lesson using a projection system. Work with students to focus on one type of error at a time, correcting all errors of the same type (e.g., capitalization, commas, subject/verb agreement, spelling). Refer to the Error Summary in the Editing Key to help you identify the various types of errors.

Option 3

Conduct a mini-lesson on one or more of the skills emphasized in that day's lesson—for example, run-on sentences or commas to separate coordinate adjectives. This is especially appropriate for new or unfamiliar skills, or for skills that are especially challenging or confusing for students (such as misplaced or dangling modifiers). After introducing a specific skill, use the approach outlined in Option 2 to focus on that skill in one or more of the week's daily paragraphs. To provide additional practice, refer to the Skills Scope and Sequence (pages 9 and 10) to find other compositions that include that target skill.

Individual Practice

Once students are familiar with the process for editing the daily paragraphs, they may work on their own or with a partner to make corrections. Be sure students have the Proofreading Marks page available to help them mark their corrections. Remind students to refer to the student Language Handbook as needed for guidance in the rules of mechanics and usage. Some students may find it helpful to know at the outset the number and types of errors they are seeking. Provide this information by referring to the Error Summary on the annotated Editing Key pages.

Customizing Instruction

Some of the skills covered in *Daily Paragraph Editing* may not be part of the grade-level expectancies in the language program you use. Some skills may even be taught differently in your program from the way they are modeled in *Daily Paragraph Editing*. In such cases, follow the approach used in your program. Simply revise the paragraph text as needed (using correction fluid or tape and then writing changes) before you reproduce pages for students.

Occasionally, you or your students may make a correction that differs from that shown in the Editing Key. The decision to use an exclamation mark instead of a period, or a period instead of a semicolon, is often a subjective decision made by individual writers. When discrepancies of this sort arise, capitalize on the "teachable moment" to let students know that there are gray areas in English usage and mechanics, and discuss how each of the possible correct choices can affect the meaning or tone of the writing.

Using the Writing Prompts

Have students keep their daily lessons in a folder so they can review the week's corrected paragraphs on Friday. Present the Friday writing prompt using a projection system, or distribute copies to students. Identify for students the writing form modeled in the composition and any of its special features (e.g., dialogue in fiction, an opinion statement in a persuasive essay, or a salutation in a letter). Take a few minutes to brainstorm ideas with the group and to focus on language skills that students will need to address in their writing.

After students have completed their writing, encourage them to use an editing checklist (see page 8 for ideas) to review or revise their work. You may also want to have partners review each other's writing. To conduct a more formal assessment of students' writing, use the Assessment Rubric on page 11.

If you assign paragraph writing as homework, make sure that students have the daily lessons (with corrections) for that week available for reference. Students may need to reflect on the content as well as the form to complete the writing assignment.

Creating an Editing Checklist

You may want to develop an editing checklist with the class. Post the checklist in the classroom and encourage students to use it as they revise their own writing or critique a partner's efforts. Here are some items for your checklist:

- Does each proper noun begin with a capital letter?
- Does each sentence end with a period, a question mark, or an exclamation point?
- Did I use an apostrophe correctly in a contraction?
- Did I use an apostrophe correctly to show possession?
- Did I place commas where they are needed?
- Did I use the correct word of two or more homonyms?
- Does the verb in each sentence agree with the subject?
- Are my sentences clear and complete?
- Are there any spelling errors?

Assessment Rubric for Evaluating Friday Paragraph Writing

The Friday writing prompts give students the opportunity to apply the capitalization, punctuation, and language usage skills they practiced during the week's editing tasks. They also require students to write in a variety of forms.

In evaluating the Friday paragraphs, you may want to focus exclusively on students' mastery of mechanics and usage, or you may want to conduct a more global assessment of their writing. The rubric on page 11 offers broad guidelines for evaluating the composition as a whole. You may want to share the rubric with students so they know what is expected of them.

Daily Paragraph Editing • EMC 2838 • © Evan-Moor Corp.

Skills Scope and Sequence

Weeks

Capitalization

Skill	1	2	3	4	5	6	7	8	9	10	11	12	13	14	15	16	17	18	19	20	21	22	23	24	25	26	27	28	29	30	31	32	33	34	35	36
Beginning of sentences, quotations, salutations/closings	●	●	●	●	●	●	●	●	●	●	●	●	●	●	●	●	●	●	●	●	●	●	●	●	●	●	●	●	●	●	●	●	●	●	●	●
Days and months			●			●					●										●					●					●					
Holidays, historic events, eras, historical documents																		●		●					●											
Inappropriate capitalization	●	●		●		●			●	●	●		●	●	●	●	●		●	●						●	●					●	●			●
Initials, acronyms, abbreviations, headings	●				●	●			●					●			●									●								●	●	●
Names and titles, languages, nationalities, geographic identities	●	●		●								●						●							●								●	●		●
Nouns used as names (Aunt, Grandpa, etc.)								●															●									●		●		
Place names, organizations, other proper nouns			●	●			●								●						●											●	●			●
Titles of books, magazines, stories, movies, TV shows				●								●				●																		●		

Language Usage

Skill	1	2	3	4	5	6	7	8	9	10	11	12	13	14	15	16	17	18	19	20	21	22	23	24	25	26	27	28	29	30	31	32	33	34	35	36
Adverbs	●	●	●	●	●	●	●	●	●	●	●	●	●	●	●	●	●	●	●	●	●	●	●	●	●	●	●	●	●	●	●	●	●	●	●	●
Articles	●	●	●	●	●	●																														●
Commonly mistaken words (affect/effect, then/than, etc.)	●									●									●							●							●			
Comparative and superlative forms					●									●															●							●
Inappropriate double negatives	●		●					●								●																				
Pronouns and possessives (its, our, whose, etc.)	●			●	●	●			●		●		●						●				●		●		●			●		●		●		●
Subject-verb agreement and plural usage	●	●	●	●	●	●	●		●	●		●	●			●		●		●		●	●	●	●	●	●	●		●	●	●	●		●	●
Verbs and verb tenses, including irregular and passive forms	●																																			

Punctuation: Apostrophes

Skill	1	2	3	4	5	6	7	8	9	10	11	12	13	14	15	16	17	18	19	20	21	22	23	24	25	26	27	28	29	30	31	32	33	34	35	36
To form contractions	●	●			●	●	●		●	●		●					●	●				●	●			●	●	●			●	●	●	●		●
To form possessives	●	●	●	●	●	●			●	●	●					●						●	●				●				●				●	●
Improperly placed apostrophes	●	●																																	●	

Punctuation: Commas

Skill	1	2	3	4	5	6	7	8	9	10	11	12	13	14	15	16	17	18	19	20	21	22	23	24	25	26	27	28	29	30	31	32	33	34	35	36
After introductory interjections or expressions	●	●			●	●			●					●								●				●		●				●				●
After introductory words or phrases	●	●											●				●				●												●			●
After salutation and closing in a letter				●				●											●						●											
Between city and state, city and country names	●																●			●							●		●							●
Between items in a series	●	●	●	●	●	●	●	●	●	●	●		●							●		●	●	●			●		●		●	●		●	●	●
Improperly placed comma	●	●	●	●	●	●			●					●										●								●			●	●
In complex sentences	●			●	●																			●										●	●	●
In compound sentences	●		●	●	●																				●								●		●	●
In dates										●		●					●		●					●						●						
To separate coordinate adjectives																			●		●											●			●	●
To set off appositives				●							●																						●			●

Skills Scope and Sequence (continued)

Weeks

	1	2	3	4	5	6	7	8	9	10	11	12	13	14	15	16	17	18	19	20	21	22	23	24	25	26	27	28	29	30	31	32	33	34	35	36
Punctuation: Commas (continued)																																				
To set off interruptions	●	●	●					●									●	●				●							●					●	●	
To set off participial phrases			●			●					●																●									
To set off quotations				●		●														●						●						●	●		●	
With name used in direct address				●																						●						●				●
Punctuation: Periods																																				
At end of sentence	●	●	●	●	●	●	●	●	●	●	●	●	●	●	●	●	●	●	●	●	●	●	●	●	●	●	●	●	●	●	●	●	●	●	●	●
Improperly placed period			●	●	●	●			●	●	●	●	●	●	●			●	●	●	●	●	●	●	●	●	●			●	●	●	●	●	●	●
In abbreviations of names, measurements, scientific names, etc.	●				●					●						●										●		●				●				
Punctuation: Quotation Marks																																				
Improperly placed quotation mark			●														●															●			●	●
In dialogue, speech, excerpts		●				●							●												●							●				●
To set apart special words or phrases	●				●		●	●	●			●								●						●						●				
With titles of articles, poems, short stories, songs, etc.									●					●																						●
Punctuation: Other																																				
Colon	●								●																											
Dash to set off a word, to show a break, etc.			●		●											●						●		●		●					●		●	●		
Ellipses for pause or omission		●																							●											●
Exclamation point	●											●			●			●		●	●							●				●				
Hyphen to form adjectives, spelled-out numbers, etc.	●	●	●		●									●	●											●		●	●		●	●		●		●
Improperly placed hyphen	●														●													●								
Parentheses and brackets	●	●			●		●	●			●				●									●					●		●		●			
Punctuation inside quotation marks			●		●	●	●					●														●					●	●				●
Punctuation with parentheses or brackets											●													●			●		●			●				
Question mark		●				●											●		●	●										●	●	●				
Semicolon to join two independent clauses	●	●																●	●									●								
Underline scientific names, foreign words, ship names, etc.					●		●												●								●									
Underline titles of books, magazines, movies, newspapers, etc.				●																					●									●		
Sentence Structure																																				
Misplaced and dangling modifiers																										●					●	●				●
Parallel structure							●						●								●									●					●	
Spelling																																				
Identify errors in grade-level words	●	●	●	●	●	●	●	●	●	●	●	●	●	●	●	●	●	●	●	●	●	●	●	●	●	●	●	●	●	●	●	●	●	●	●	●

Assessment Rubric

	EXCELLENT	GOOD	FAIR	WEAK
Clarity and Focus	Writing is exceptionally clear, focused, and interesting.	Writing is generally clear, focused, and interesting.	Writing is loosely focused on the topic.	Writing is unclear and unfocused.
Development of Main Ideas	Main ideas are clear, specific, and well developed.	Main ideas are identifiable but may be somewhat general.	Main ideas are overly broad or simplistic.	Main ideas are unclear or not expressed.
Organization	Organization is clear (beginning, middle, and end) and fits the topic and writing form.	Organization is clear but may be predictable or formulaic.	Organization is attempted but is often unclear.	Organization is not coherent.
Use of Details	Details are relevant, specific, and well placed.	Details are relevant but may be overly general.	Details may be off-topic, predictable, or not specific enough.	Details are absent or insufficient to support main ideas.
Vocabulary	Vocabulary is exceptionally rich, varied, and well chosen.	Vocabulary is colorful and generally avoids clichés.	Vocabulary is ordinary and may rely on clichés.	Vocabulary is limited, general, or vague.
Mechanics and Usage	Demonstrates exceptionally strong command of conventions of punctuation, capitalization, spelling, and usage.	Demonstrates adequate control of conventions of punctuation, capitalization, spelling, and usage.	Errors in the conventions of mechanics and language usage distract but do not impede the reader.	Limited ability to control conventions of mechanics and language usage impairs readability of the composition.

MONDAY   Week 1

John Carter of Mars

Captain john carter, the main character in a series of fanntasie [fantasy] novels by Edgar Rice burroughs, is the perfect romantic Hero. Originally from virginia Carter is a courteous man of good character—but he is not to be trifled with. He will quick [quickly] draw his sword and fight to the death for what he believe [believes] in he is pursistant [persistent], rugged strong and imortal [immortal]. Carter cannot recall having had a childhood; he has always been about 30 years old and never ages. One day, while searching for Gold in a [an] arizona cave, he "dies" unexpectidly [unexpectedly] . . or does he? Carter awakens to find himself on mars.

Error Summary

Capitalization	9
Language Usage	3
Punctuation:	
Comma	3
Ellipses	1
Hyphen	1
Period	1
Question Mark	1
Spelling	4

TUESDAY   Week 1

On Mars (which the Martians call "Barsoom), Carter quickly recognize [recognizes] that his advanced sword skills, and his extra ordinary strength are useful to him. He adapt [adapts] to the turbulent barsoomian environment which is chaotic due to frequent wars between regions. He doesnt waste no time in displaying his fearce [fierce] determination and strength. In fact, his earthly strength is intensified on barsoom because of the lower gravvaty [gravity] (and lower resistance to movemint [movement] on mars. After killing a martian cheif [chief] and taking over a tribe of warriors, Carter become [becomes] a warlord, whose primary goal is to make life better for Barsooms inhabitants

Error Summary

Capitalization	4
Language Usage	4
Punctuation:	
Apostrophe	2
Comma	2
Parentheses	1
Period	1
Quotation Mark	1
Spelling	5

Name _____

John Carter of Mars

Captain john carter, the main character in a series of fanntasie novels by Edgar Rice burroughs, is the perfect romantic Hero. Originally from virginia Carter is a courteous man of good character—but he is not to be trifled with. He will quick draw his sword and fight to the death for what he believe in he is pursistant, rugged strong and imortal. Carter cannot recall having had a childhood; he has always been about 30 years-old and never ages. One day, while searching for Gold in a arizona cave, he "dies" unexpectidly . . or does he Carter awakens to find himself on mars.

- personal names
- adverbs
- hyphens
- run-on sentences
- ellipses

On Mars (which the Martians call "Barsoom), Carter quickly recognize that his advanced sword skills, and his extra ordinary strength are useful to him. He adapt to the turbulent barsoomian environment which is chaotic due to frequent wars between regions. He doesnt waste no time in displaying his fearce determination and strength. In fact, his earthly strength is intensified on barsoom because of the lower gravvaty (and lower resistance to movemint on mars. After killing a martian cheif and taking over a tribe of warriors, Carter become a warlord, whose primary goal is to make life better for Barsooms inhabitants

- geographic identities
- verbs
- double negatives

WEDNESDAY   Week 1

Carter has many heroic adventures on barsoom. in one
story, he witness the capture of a alien princess named dejah
by some big green martians with who he keeps company.
Being an honoruble gentleman (after all he's from Virginia),
captain carter resolve to help poor Dejah escapes her
Martian captors and protect her verchue. Even after this
initial escape, Dejah is frequently the target of evil villains,
whom Carter must protects her from. Carter will never
despair or back down from a fight. He always knows in the
back of his mind that he will win the fight. Because of his
great strength, and swordsmanship.

Editing marks indicate: witnesses · an · whom · honorable · resolves · escape · virtue · protect

Error Summary

Capitalization	7
Language Usage	6
Punctuation:	
Comma	3
Period	2
Spelling	2

THURSDAY   Week 1

Carter is the kind of person that you would want on
your side if you found yourself in a scuffle. Hes the kind of
person that everyone want to cheer for. he's so good that
his enemies simply must be considered bad. Judjing from his
adventures though, this hero is easily provoaked into fatal
combat. The character of the courteous, well-mannered
captain Carter is transformed when ever princess Dejah is
under threat; than he becomes a ruthless vindicator, fixed
on revenje. Eventually, Carter marries Dejah and serves as
warlord hero and dutiful family man on mars. Occasionally he
returns to Earth, though, to tell about his aventures.

Editing marks indicate: wants · Judging · provoked · then · revenge · Occasionally · adventures

Error Summary

Capitalization	4
Language Usage	2
Punctuation:	
Apostrophe	1
Comma	3
Hyphen	1
Period	1
Spelling	6

WEDNESDAY   Week 1

Carter has many heroic adventures on barsoom, in one story, he witness the capture of a alien princess named dejah by some big green martians with who he keeps company. Being an honoruble gentleman (after all he's from Virginia), captain carter resolve to help poor Dejah escapes her Martian captors and protect her verchue. Even after this initial escape, Dejah is frequently the target of evil villains, whom Carter must protects her from. Carter will never despair or back down from a fight. He always knows in the back of his mind that he will win the fight. Because of his great strength, and swordsmanship.

WATCH FOR

- run-on sentences
- pronouns
- commas
- incomplete sentences

THURSDAY   Week 1

Carter is the kind of person that you would want on your side if you found yourself in a scuffle. Hes the kind of person that everyone want to cheer for, he's so good that his enemies simply must be considered bad. Judjing from his adventures though, this hero is easily provoaked into fatal combat. The character of the courteous, well mannered captain Carter is transformed when ever princess Dejah is under threat; than he becomes a ruthless vindicator, fixed on revenje. Eventually, Carter marries Dejah and serves as warlord hero and dutiful family man on mars. Ocasionally he returns to Earth, though, to tell about his aventures.

WATCH FOR

- run-on sentences
- hyphens
- titles of people
- commas

MONDAY   Week 2

Common Superstitions

A superstition is a commonly held belief, that may or may not be supported by facts. People in all parts of the world holds [hold] such beliefs one well-known souperstition [superstition] involve [involves] pennies, and it go [goes] like this: "Find a penny, pick it up; all day long, youll [you'll] have good luck. A pesible [possible] origin of this superstition are [is] the anceint [ancient] belief that gods gave mettal [metal] to humans to protect them from evil. Pennies is [are] made of metal, which is why they are considered to bring luck. However, some people say, that its [it's] only lucky to find a heads-up penny and that an [a] heads-down penny brings bad luck.

Error Summary

Capitalization	1
Language Usage	6
Punctuation:	
Apostrophe	2
Comma	2
Hyphen	2
Period	2
Quotation Mark	1
Spelling	4

TUESDAY   Week 2

Another commin [common] superstition is that braking [breaking] a mirror, brings seven years of bad luck. The origin of this belief go [goes] back to ancient roman times. The Romans were the first to create mirrers [mirrors] made of glass. They believe [believed] that a mirror could capchure [capture] part of the sole [soul] of anyone who looked into it. Breaking the mirror, then, would shatter the persons [person's] soul, which would cause the person's health to deekline [decline]. So it would take seven year's [years] for the person's health to reecover [recover]. why seven years? According to ancient lore, the human body and soul is [are] renewed every seven years. While waiting, the person would be unable, to deflect bad luck.

Error Summary

Capitalization	2
Language Usage	3
Punctuation:	
Apostrophe	2
Comma	3
Question Mark	1
Spelling	7

Name _____

Common Superstitions

A superstition is a commonly held belief, that may or may not be supported by facts. People in all parts of the world holds such beliefs one well known souperstition involve pennies, and it go like this: "Find a penny, pick it up; all day long, youll have good luck. A posible origin of this superstition are the anceint belief that gods gave mettal to humans to protect them from evil. Pennies is made of metal, which is why they are considered to bring luck. However, some people say, that its only lucky to find a heads-up penny and that an heads down penny brings bad luck

WATCH FOR

- verbs
- quotation marks
- end punctuation
- hyphens

Another commin superstition is that braking a mirror, brings seven years of bad luck. The origin of this belief go back to ancient roman times. The Romans were the first to create mirrers made of glass. They believe that a mirror could capchure part of the sole of anyone who looked into it. Breaking the mirror, then, would shatter the persons soul, which would cause the person's health to deekline. So it would take seven year's for the person's health to reecover. why seven years According to ancient lore the human body and soul is renewed every seven years. While waiting, the person would be unable, to deflect bad luck.

WATCH FOR

- commas
- nationalities
- apostrophes
- run-on sentences

WEDNESDAY　　　　　　　　　　　　　　Week 2

    <u>m</u>any ~~moddern~~ [modern] superstitions, relate to ~~cazsual~~ [casual] events.
You may ~~of~~ [have] heard, for example, that if your ears redden, it
means people somewhere ~~is~~ [are] talking about you. Supposedly,
blowing away a fallen ~~eyeslash~~ [eyelash] can make your wish come true.
Another ~~S~~uperstition claims that plucking one gray hair will
cause ten more to grow in it~~'~~s place. There are superstitions
about ~~snezing~~ [sneezing], too. [An] A old [e]nglish belief says that sneezing
three times before breakfast means you'll get exciting news.
In [j]apan, sneezing unexpectedly means that someone far away
is talking about you. sneezing twice in [a] ~~an~~ short period of
time ~~mean~~ [means] that the person is saying bad things about you.

Error Summary

Capitalization	5
Language Usage	5
Punctuation:	
Apostrophe	2
Comma	2
Period	2
Spelling	4

THURSDAY　　　　　　　　　　　　　　Week 2

    Good or [B]ad luck ~~are~~ [is] often the focus of superstitions—
[f]or example, having bad luck from opening [an] a umbrella indoors
or good luck from finding a four-leaf clover (especially if you
find it ~~axidentally~~ [accidentally]). Catching a falling leaf on the first day of
[autumn] ~~autumm~~ is considered lucky; it means that you won't catch a
cold all winter. Likewise, [an] a itchy palm ~~foreshaddows~~ [foreshadows] good luck;
it ~~suggest~~ [suggests] that you will soon ~~recieve~~ [receive] money. According to
some people, stepping on your own shadow ~~bring~~ [brings] good luck.
Some people try to ~~attracts~~ [attract] good luck by carrying a lucky
charm. Even if you don't believe in superstition, it's ~~temting~~ [tempting] to
follow superstitious practices—just in case.

Error Summary

Capitalization	2
Language Usage	6
Punctuation:	
Apostrophe	3
Hyphen	1
Parentheses	1
Semicolon	1
Spelling	5

18

Name _____

WEDNESDAY   Week 2

many moddern superstitions, relate to cazsual events. You may of heard, for example that if your ears redden, it means people somewhere is talking about you. Supposedly, blowing away a fallen eyeslash can make your wish come true. Another Superstition claims that plucking one gray hair will cause ten more to grow in it's place. There are superstitions about snezing, too A old english belief says that sneezing three times before breakfast means youll get exciting news. In japan, sneezing unexpectedly means that someone far away is talking about you, sneezing twice in an short period of time mean that the person is saying bad things about you.

- run-on sentences
- nationalities
- place names

THURSDAY   Week 2

Good or Bad luck are often the focus of superstitions— For example, having bad luck from opening a umbrella indoors or good luck from finding a four leaf clover especially if you find it axidentally). Catching a falling leaf on the first day of autumm is considered lucky; it means that you wont catch a cold all winter. Likewise, a itchy palm foreshaddows good luck it suggest that you will soon recieve money. According to some people, stepping on your own shadow bring good luck. Some people try to attracts good luck by carrying a lucky charm. Even if you dont believe in superstition, its temting to follow superstitious practices—just in case.

- verbs
- hyphens
- parentheses
- semicolons

MONDAY   Week 3

Are Fake Lawns the Answer?

It's saturday morning on a warm, summer day. You'd like nothing better than to sleep late. Instead, you have to crawl out of bed, start the lawn mower, and follow the noisy machine around the yard. As it throws off bits of grass in all directions. This is a ~~familair~~ *familiar* scenario in ~~subburben~~ *suburban* neighborhoods across the united States. Especially for teens who ~~dred~~ *dread* the weekly sneeze-inducing task of mowing the lawn. Lush green lawns are nice, but maintaining them takes time, And wastes ~~recources~~ *resources*. A high-quality artificial lawn looks just as ~~well~~ *good* as a real lawn, and never needs mowing.

Error Summary

Capitalization	6
Language Usage	1
Punctuation:	
Apostrophe	2
Comma	6
Hyphen	2
Period	3
Spelling	4

TUESDAY   Week 3

People say that ~~artifishul~~ *artificial* lawns are unnatural. ~~Ironicly~~ *Ironically*, fake turf ~~are~~ *is* friendlier to the ~~enviroment~~ *environment* than real grass. To stay green and ~~helthy~~ *healthy* lawns need a great deal of water, as well as fertilizer and ~~pestasides~~ *pesticides*. On average, they need at least ~~a~~ *an* inch of water per week during the growing season. You could even say that "lawns seem frivolous," given the ~~shortidge~~ *shortage* of usable water in the world. Also, a lawn may need as much as four pounds of high-nitrogen fertilizer per 1,000 sq ft each year. most lawn fertilizers ~~is~~ *are* made from chemicals, which runoff water ~~carry~~ *carries* into lakes and streams. Thereby ~~contaminating~~ *contaminating* the water supply.

Error Summary

Capitalization	2
Language Usage	4
Punctuation:	
Comma	2
Hyphen	1
Period	2
Quotation Mark	2
Spelling	7

       Daily Paragraph Editing • EMC 2838 • © Evan-Moor Corp.

Name _____

- hyphens
- incomplete sentences
- adjectives

Are Fake Lawns the Answer?

Its saturday morning on a warm, Summer day. Youd like nothing better than to sleep late. Instead, you have to crawl out of bed start the lawn mower and follow the noisy machine around the yard. As it throws off bits of grass in all directions. This is a familair scenario in subburben neighborhoods across the united States. Especially for teens who dred the weekly sneeze inducing task of mowing the lawn. Lush green lawns are nice but maintaining them takes time. And wastes recources. A high quality artificial lawn looks just as well as a real lawn, and never needs mowing

- verbs
- hyphens
- commas
- abbreviations

People say that artifishul lawns are unnatural. Ironicly, fake turf are friendlier to the enviroment than real grass. To stay green and helthy lawns need a great deal of water, as well as fertilizer and pestasides. On average, they need at least a inch of water per week during the growing season. You could even say that "lawns seem frivolous," given the shortidge of usable water in the world. Also, a lawn may need as much as four pounds of high nitrogen fertilizer per 1,000 sq ft each year. most lawn fertilizers is made from chemicals, which runoff water carry into lakes and streams. Thereby contamminating the water supply.

WEDNESDAY   Week 3

Then there's the issue of lawn mower's. Lawns generally
need
~~needs~~ to be cut once a week to stay healthy. Lawn mowers,
whether gas or electric contribute to Noise Pollution. Even
manual
~~manuel~~ ones (that is, push mowers) can be ~~anoiying~~ **annoying** and can
disturb
~~disterb~~ peaceful summer days. Moreover gas and electric
pollute
mowers ~~pullute~~ the air. According to the U.S. environmental
protection agency or EPA, gas-powered lawn mowers ~~produces~~ **produce**
five per cent of the smog in some areas. Electric-powered
mowers are less harmful. But still use energy. Imagine how
much energy we'd save. If homes and parks ~~instauled~~ **installed** fake
turf instead of sod!

Error Summary

Capitalization	7
Language Usage	2
Punctuation:	
Apostrophe	2
Comma	4
Hyphen	2
Parentheses	1
Period	2
Spelling	6

THURSDAY   Week 3

advantages
Artificial lawns have many ~~advanteges~~ over natural
ever
lawns. You won't ~~never~~ have to water them, cut them, or
them
fertilize ~~it~~. Dandelions crabgrass and other weeds wont take
over. And you won't have to spray weedkillers, which harm
beneficial insects birds and other animals. Artificial lawns,
concrete
have advantages over brick ~~concreet~~ and other hard surfaces,
They're
too. ~~Their~~ softer to walk on and won't skin your hands and
They   **through**
knees if you fall down. ~~It~~ also let rain seep ~~threw~~ to fill the
grumble
water table. Some people ~~grummble~~ that fake grass doesn't
give that fresh-cut grass smell. To those people, I say,
"Sneeze if you want to, but count me out!"

Error Summary

Language Usage	3
Punctuation:	
Apostrophe	2
Comma	7
Period	2
Spelling	5

WEDNESDAY   Week 3

        Then theres the issue of lawn mower's. Lawns generally
needs to be cut once a week to stay healthy. Lawn mowers,
whether gas or electric contribute to Noise Pollution. Even
manuel ones (that is, push mowers can be anoiying, and can
disterb peaceful summer days. Moreover gas and electric
mowers pullute the air. According to the U.S. environmental
protection agency or EPA, gas powered lawn mowers produces
five per cent of the smog in some areas. Electric powered
mowers are less harmful. But still use energy. Imagine how
much energy we'd save. If homes and parks instauled fake
turf instead of sod!

- commas
- names of organizations
- parentheses
- incomplete sentences
- hyphens

THURSDAY   Week 3

        Artificial lawns have many advanteges over natural
lawns. You won't never have to water them, cut them, or
fertilize it. Dandelions crabgrass and other weeds wont take
over And you won't have to spray weedkillers, which harm
beneficial insects birds and other animals. Artificial lawns,
have advantages over brick concreet and other hard surfaces,
too. Their softer to walk on and won't skin your hands and
knees if you fall down. It also let rain seep threw to fill the
water table. Some people grummble that fake grass doesnt
give that fresh-cut grass smell. To those people, I say,
"Sneeze if you want to, but count me out!".

- double negatives
- pronouns
- commas

MONDAY   Week 4

To Kill a Mockingbird

To Kill a mockingbird, a book by harper Lee tells the
story of Atticus Finch, an ~~aturney~~ attorney and widowed father in the
small town of Maycomb alabama and his children, Scout and
Jem. The novel is set in the 1930s Atticus agrees to defend
Tom Robinson, a African American who is ~~wrongful~~ wrongfully ~~ackused~~ accused of
a crime against a white woman. Because of atticus's actions
his children are exposed for the first time to the racial
~~prejudis~~ prejudice and hypocrisy of their small, southern town. However
the decision also ~~provide~~ provides Scout (who narrates the story) with
a ~~valuble~~ valuable learning experience

Error Summary

Capitalization	4
Language Usage	3
Punctuation:	
Comma	7
Parentheses	1
Period	2
Underlined Words	4
Spelling	4

TUESDAY   Week 4

Atticus defends the ~~innasent~~ innocent Tom Robinson but Scout
and jem ~~faces~~ face abuse from residents of maycomb as a result.
The young children hear slurs toward their father, and are
provoked to fight for his honor. Scout and Jem, meanwhile,
become obsessed with their ~~misteerious~~ mysterious neighbor, Boo radley
~~who~~ whom they hear terrible rumors about (rumors they believe
at first). ~~Evantualy~~ Eventually, scout and Jem stop believing the rumors.
Later Boo saves the children from ~~a~~ an attacker (someone ~~whom~~ who
becomes angry with Atticus at the trial) Even though Atticus
proves that Tom could not have committed the crime the
members of the jury ~~ignores~~ ignore the ~~evadense~~ evidence and ~~convicts~~ convict Tom.

Error Summary

Capitalization	4
Language Usage	6
Punctuation:	
Comma	5
Parentheses	2
Spelling	4

MONDAY   Week 4

To Kill a Mockingbird

To Kill a mockingbird, a book by harper Lee tells the story of Atticus Finch, an aturney and widowed father in the small town of Maycomb alabama and his children, Scout and Jem. The novel is set in the 1930s Atticus agrees to defend Tom Robinson a African American who is wrongful ackused of a crime against a white woman. Because of atticus's actions his children are exposed for the first time to the racial prejudis and hypocrisy of their small, southern town. However the decision also provide Scout (who narrates the story with a valuble learning experience

WATCH FOR

- book titles
- personal names
- run-on sentences
- adverbs

TUESDAY   Week 4

Atticus defends the innasent Tom Robinson but Scout and jem faces abuse from residents of maycomb as a result. The young children hear slurs toward their father, and are provoked to fight for his honor. Scout and Jem, meanwhile, become obsessed with their misteerious neighbor, Boo radley who they hear terrible rumors about (rumors they believe at first. Evantualy, scout and Jem stop believing the rumors. Later Boo saves the children from a attacker (someone whom becomes angry with Atticus at the trial.) Even though Atticus proves that Tom could not have committed the crime the members of the jury ignores the evadense and convicts Tom.

WATCH FOR

- personal names
- commas
- pronouns
- punctuation with parentheses

WEDNESDAY   Week 4

An important theme in <u>To Kill</u> a <u>mockingbird</u> is that prejudice can lead to ~~injustous~~ injustice. When Atticus defends Tom, Scout and Jem become aware that unfair things happen in the world. They see how prejudice cloud's peoples judgment, And how the townspeople support the Jurys ~~virdict~~ verdict. They also see that the legal system can fail to be fair.

Another theme is the struggle for ~~morrality~~ morality. Scout contemplates how people decide what is right And what is wrong. She recognizes her father's reason for taking Toms case despite the ~~likelyhood~~ likelihood that he will not win: Atticus simply thinks that it is the right thing to do.

Error Summary

Capitalization	5
Punctuation:	
Apostrophe	5
Comma	1
Period	3
Underlined Words	4
Spelling	4

THURSDAY   Week 4

From the beginning of the book, Scout proves to be a ~~acceptionally~~ an exceptionally thoughtful and ~~observent~~ observant child but her views evolve as the story progresses. She starts out as a playful tom boy, but her world changes when she is ~~expozed~~ exposed to ~~rayshel~~ racial inequality. She ~~identify~~ identifies unfairness in her world and ~~see~~ sees it ~~pracktised~~ practiced by adults around her. Scout also learns by observation that people have the ~~cappasity~~ capacity to do just as much good as bad. By a the end of the book, she has learned to consult her own ~~conshunce~~ conscience to decide what is right or wrong. As Lees book teaches us "The one thing that doesnt abide by majority rule is a persons conscience".

Error Summary

Language Usage	4
Punctuation:	
Apostrophe	3
Comma	2
Quotation Mark	1
Spelling	8

WEDNESDAY   Week 4

An important theme in To kill A mockingbird is that prejudice can lead to injustous. When Atticus defends Tom Scout and Jem become aware that unfair things happen in the world. They see how prejudice cloud's peoples judgment. And how the townspeople support the Jurys virdict. They also see that the legal system can fail to be fair

Another theme is the struggle for morrality. Scout contemplates how people decide what is right. And what is wrong. She recognizes her fathers reason for taking Toms case despite the likelyhood that he will not win: Atticus simply thinks that it is the right thing to do.

WATCH FOR

- book titles
- incomplete sentences
- apostrophes

THURSDAY   Week 4

From the beginning of the book, Scout proves to be a acceptionally thoughtful and observent child but her views evolve as the story progresses. She starts out as a playful tom boy, but her world changes when she is expozed to rayshel inequality. She identify unfairness in her world and see it pracktised by adults around her. Scout also learns by observation that people have the cappasity to do just as much good as bad. By a end of the book, she has learned to consult her own conshunce to decide what is right or wrong. As Lees book teaches us "The one thing that doesnt abide by majority rule is a persons conscience".

WATCH FOR

- articles
- compound words
- punctuation with quotation marks

MONDAY   Week 5

The Black Death

        difference   *an*

The ~~diffrence~~ between a ~~E~~pidemic and a ~~P~~andemic is
the distance *they* ~~it~~ cover. An epidemic is a *contagious* ~~contajous~~ disease,
that *spreads* ~~spread~~ throughout a community. A pandemic, on the
other hand, spreads over a *larger* ~~more large~~ area, sometimes *across* ~~acrost~~
many countries. Based on these *definitions* ~~defenitions~~, we can categorize
the "Black Death," which devastated ~~e~~urope in the 1300s, as a
pandemic. By the time it ended, it had killed about 25 million
people—roughly a third of Europe's population. This terrible
disease ~~diseese~~, also called the plague, *began* ~~begun~~ in ~~a~~sia and was brought
to Europe through *an* ~~a~~ act of ~~W~~ar.

Error Summary

Capitalization	5
Language Usage	6
Punctuation:	
Apostrophe	1
Comma	5
Dash	1
Quotation Mark	1
Spelling	5

TUESDAY   Week 5

Invaders ~~Invaiders~~ trying to take over a trading post in the
Crimea (a region that is now part of ~~u~~kraine) decided to try
a type of germ warfare. They used a catapult (an ancient
but effective *weapon* ~~weapan~~) to fling plague-ridden corpses into the
town. the disease quickly spread throughout the town and
from there to ~~e~~uropean ports along the ~~m~~editerranean Sea,
creeping as far ~~N~~orth as ~~s~~candinavia. At the time, *medical* ~~medikul~~
practitioners did not know what caused the disease, and
they had no *medicines* ~~medasines~~ to combat it. We *know* ~~no~~ today that a
rod-shaped bacterium called Yersinia pestis (*abbreviated* ~~abreviated~~ as
Y. pestis) *causes* ~~cause~~ the disease.

Error Summary

Capitalization	6
Language Usage	1
Punctuation:	
Comma	2
Hyphen	2
Parentheses	2
Period	1
Spelling	6

Name _____

The Black Death

The diffrence between a Epidemic and a Pandemic is the distance it cover. An epidemic is a contajous disease, that spread throughout a community. A pandemic on the other hand spreads over a more large area, sometimes acrost many countries. Based on these defenitions we can categorize the "Black Death, which devastated europe in the 1300s, as a pandemic. By the time it ended it had killed about 25 million people roughly a third of Europes population. This terrible diseese, also called the plague, begun in asia and was brought to Europe through a act of War.

WATCH FOR

- pronouns
- commas
- place names
- dashes

Invaiders trying to take over a trading post in the Crimea (a region that is now part of ukraine decided to try a type of germ warfare. They used a catapult (an ancient but effective weapan) to fling plague ridden corpses into the town, the disease quickly spread throughout the town and from there to european ports along the mediterranean Sea, creeping as far North as scandinavia. At the time medikul practitioners did not know what caused the disease and they had no medasines to combat it. We no today that a rod shaped bacterium called <u>Yersinia</u> <u>pestis</u> (abreviated as <u>Y</u>. <u>pestis</u> cause the disease.

WATCH FOR

- hyphens
- run-on sentences
- place names
- scientific names

WEDNESDAY   Week 5

The most recent ~~G~~lobal ~~O~~utbreak of plague ~~begins~~ began in china in 1855 and continued until 1959. It was during that outbreak—in 1894, to be exact—that researchers in hong kong discovered Y. pestis. Years later, chinese doctors ~~make~~ made a critical observation that ~~link~~ linked rats, humans and fleas. They noticed that rats had plague ~~symptems,~~ symptoms that were ~~similiar~~ similar to those in people who were infected. They also noticed that humans, who had the plague, often had bites from fleas. They learned that the disease ~~genrally~~ generally is ~~transmit~~ transmitted to humans by way of a bite from the rat flea, Xenopsylla cheopis. With this information scientists ~~scientusts~~ had a starting point for a cure.

Error Summary
Capitalization	6
Language Usage	4
Punctuation:	
Comma	5
Underlined Words	4
Spelling	4

THURSDAY   Week 5

There are three different forms of plague, but Y. Pestis causes all three. Bubonic plague is the ~~commonest~~ most common form. Victims get buboes, which are ~~inlarjd~~ enlarged (and extremely sore) lymph nodes. Buboes appear around the armpit, groin, or neck. Bubonic plague is fatal in half of the cases of untreated ~~infektion~~ infection. Outbreaks of Plague still ~~occurs~~ occur in many countries, including China, mongolia, india, vietnam, and the united states. The ~~survivel~~ survival rate, however, has improved in recent years. When people get the right antibiotics in time, they ~~usual~~ usually survive. Good ~~hygeene,~~ hygiene and pest control ~~is~~ are the best practices for preventing outbreaks of the disease.

Error Summary
Capitalization	8
Language Usage	4
Punctuation:	
Comma	8
Parentheses	1
Period	1
Underlined Words	1
Spelling	4

WEDNESDAY   Week 5

The most recent Global Outbreak of plague begins in china in 1855 and continued until 1959. It was during that outbreak—in 1894, to be exact—that researchers in hong kong discovered Y. pestis. Years later, chinese doctors make a critical observation that link rats, humans and fleas. They noticed that rats had plague symptems, that were similiar to those in people who were infected. They also noticed that humans, who had the plague, often had bites from fleas. They learned that the disease genrally is transmit to humans by way of a bite from the rat flea, Xenopsylla cheopis. With this information scientusts had a starting point for a cure.

- verbs
- scientific names
- nationalities
- commas

THURSDAY   Week 5

There are three different forms of plague, but Y Pestis causes all three. Bubonic plague is the commonest form. Victims get buboes which are inlarjd (and extremely sore lymph nodes. Buboes appear around the armpit, groin or neck. Bubonic plague is Fatal in half of the cases of untreated infektion. Outbreaks of Plague still occurs in many countries, including China mongolia india vietnam and the united states. The survivel rate, however, has improved in recent years. When people get the right antibiotics in time they usual survive. Good hygeene, and pest control is the best practices for preventing outbreaks of the disease.

- words that compare
- parentheses
- place names
- adverbs

MONDAY   Week 6

The Mysterious Guest

The guests were savoring their dinner on this humid
evening
~~evaning~~. ~~They're~~ Their gracious hosts had provided a delicious
traditional indian meal. For the first ~~coarse~~ course the ~~geusts~~ guests
enjoyed fragrant, tasty samosas and now were looking forward
to the second course, which ~~were~~ was chicken vindaloo. One of
the guest's at the table was ~~a~~ an american biologist named Amy.
She was ~~vissiting~~ visiting india for six months. To study the native
snake ~~poppulation~~ population. Her work ~~brung~~ brought amy to many areas of
the world, but India was her favorite place. She enjoyed
the people, the culture, and the food.

Error Summary

Capitalization	5
Language Usage	3
Punctuation:	
Apostrophe	1
Comma	5
Period	2
Spelling	6

TUESDAY   Week 6

The guests chatted about ~~resent~~ recent movies they had seen.
As she listened to the ~~corgiul~~ cordial conversation, Amy ~~obzurved~~ observed a
strange ~~expresion~~ expression darken the hostess's face. She watched as
the hostess quietly ~~sumoned~~ summoned the maid, and whispered in her
ear. The maids' eyes widened, and she quickly left the room.
She soon returned with a bowl of milk, which she placed
~~cawshusly~~ cautiously on the patio outside the open sliding glass doors.
Although no one else had noticed, Amy was ~~horrafide~~ horrified. She
knew that a bowl of milk often means one thing in India:
bait for a snake. She realized that there must be a
dangerous snake—perhaps a cobra—in the room.

Error Summary

Punctuation:	
Apostrophe	2
Comma	4
Spelling	7

MONDAY   Week 6

The Mysterious Guest

The guests were savoring their dinner on this humid evaning. They're gracious hosts had provided a delicious traditional indian meal. For the first coarse the geusts enjoyed fragrant tasty samosas and now were looking forward to the second course, which were chicken vindaloo. One of the guest's at the table was a american biologist named Amy She was vissiting india for six months. To study the native snake poppulation. Her work brung amy to many areas of the world but India was her favorite place. She enjoyed the people the culture and the food.

WATCH FOR

- nationalities
- place names
- incomplete sentences

TUESDAY   Week 6

The guests chatted about resent movies they had seen. As she listened to the corgiul conversation Amy obzurved a strange expresion darken the hostesss face. She watched as the hostess quietly sumoned the maid, and whispered in her ear. The maids' eyes widened, and she quickly left the room. She soon returned with a bowl of milk which she placed cawshusly on the patio outside the open sliding glass doors. Although no one else had noticed Amy was horrafide. She knew that a bowl of milk often means one thing in India: bait for a snake. She realized that there must be a dangerous snake—perhaps a cobra—in the room.

WATCH FOR

- apostrophes
- commas

WEDNESDAY   Week 6

amy also knew (new) that the bowl of milk would be use less (useless).
The commonly held belief (beleif) that snakes are attracted to milk
is (are) unfounded. Amy looked all around the room, but couldn't (could'nt)
see the snake. She realized (reelized) that there (their) was only one place it
could be: under the table.

Her first thought was (is) to jump back and warn the others'
but she knew that any sudden moves could frighten (friten) the snake
into striking. She had to find a way to give (gives) the snake time
to leave. Just then, there was a convenient (conveenyunt) lull in the
conversation. Amy calmly proposed an idea. "Let's have a
contest," she said. Every one (Everyone) agreed that it might be fun.

Error Summary

Capitalization	1
Language Usage	3
Punctuation:	
Apostrophe	2
Comma	3
Quotation Mark	2
Spelling	9

THURSDAY   Week 6

"I'll count slowly to 300. That's five minutes. Don't move
a muscle (muscel) until I reach 300—or you won't get dessert (desert)," Amy said.

The guests (guest's) sat like stone statues while Amy counted.
Just as she got to 280, she saw the snake emerge (emmerge) and
slither out the open door. It was probably attracted by the
pet mouse, which the hosts' kept in a cage on the patio.
Amy jumped up to close the sliding doors. The other guests
gasped in horror (horrer) when they saw the snake.

"Just one thing mystifies me," said Amy, turning toward
the hostess. "How did you know a snake was in the room?"

"It was crawling across my feet," replied the hostess.

Error Summary

Punctuation:	
Apostrophe	6
Comma	3
Period	1
Question Mark	1
Quotation Mark	5
Spelling	4

WEDNESDAY   Week 6

- dialogue
- verbs
- compound words

amy also new that the bowl of milk would be use less. The commonly held beleif that snakes are attracted to milk are unfounded. Amy looked all around the room, but could'nt see the snake. She reelized that their was only one place it could be: under the table.

Her first thought is to jump back and warn the other's but she knew that any sudden moves could friten the snake into striking. She had to find a way to gives the snake time to leave. Just then, there was a conveenyunt lull in the conversation. Amy calmly proposed an idea. Lets have a contest she said. Every one agreed that it might be fun.

THURSDAY   Week 6

- dialogue
- apostrophes
- end punctuation

I'll count slowly to 300. Thats five minute's. Dont move a muscel until I reach 300—or you wont get desert," Amy said.

The guest's sat like stone statues while Amy counted. Just as she got to 280, she saw the snake emmerge and slither out the open door. It was probably attracted by the pet mouse, which the hosts' kept in a cage on the patio. Amy jumped up to close the sliding doors The other guests gasped in horrer when they saw the snake.

"Just one thing mystifies me said Amy turning toward the hostess. How did you know a snake was in the room

"It was crawling across my feet replied the hostess.

MONDAY   Week 7

A Slippery Problem

Americans spend millions of dollars every year on
antibacterial soap to ~~wards~~ [ward] off harmful microbes (germs).
the [is] problem ~~are~~ that certain ~~ingridents~~ [ingredients] in ~~A~~ntibacterial soap
actually ~~leaves~~ [leave] a residue on our skin and strong germs are
able to survive in that residue. ~~Altho~~ [Although] this type of soap
~~eliminate~~ [eliminates] many ~~jerms~~ [germs], it does not get rid of all of them.
Even ~~worst~~ [worse], most antibacterial soaps use triclosan, a chemical
~~campowned~~ [compound] that could be making these strong germs even
stronger. this [=] is a problem because American's use lots and
lots of this soap.

Error Summary

Capitalization	3
Language Usage	5
Punctuation:	
Apostrophe	1
Comma	1
Parentheses	1
Period	2
Spelling	4

TUESDAY   Week 7

How do germs become ~~more strong~~ [stronger]? Cleaning with
antibacterial soap typically ~~kill~~ [kills] the ~~most weak~~ [weakest] germs, leaving
behind the most resilient ones. When those germs then
~~reproduces~~ [reproduce], they pass along certain traits to ~~there~~ [their] offspring.
The result—after many generations—~~are~~ [is] a class of strong,
"superbugs". ~~This~~ [These] obstinate germs can with stand the chemical
compound triclosan. In some cases, the bacteria can also
~~resists~~ [resist] antibiotic drug's that doctors ~~perscribe~~ [prescribe] (such as
amoxycillin) to fight infections. Bacterial ~~rezistanse~~ [resistance] to such
drugs has ~~increase~~ [increased] in recent years. the residue left behind
by antibacterial soap is largely responsible.

Error Summary

Capitalization	1
Language Usage	8
Punctuation:	
Apostrophe	1
Comma	2
Question Mark	1
Quotation Mark	1
Spelling	4

Name _____

A Slippery Problem

Americans spend millions of dollars every year on antibacterial soap to wards off harmful microbes (germs. the problem are that certain ingridents in Antibacterial soap actually leaves a residue on our skin and strong germs are able to survive in that residue. Altho this type of soap eliminate many jerms, it does not get rid of all of them. Even worst, most antibacterial soaps use triclosan, a chemical campowned that could be making these strong germs even stronger, this is a problem because American's use lots and lots of this soap

- verbs
- punctuation with parentheses
- words that compare
- run-on sentences

How do germs become more strong. Cleaning with antibacterial soap typically kill the most weak germs, leaving behind the most resilient ones. When those germs then reproduces, they pass along certain traits to there offspring. The result—after many generations—are a class of strong, "superbugs". This obstinate germs can with stand the chemical compound triclosan. In some cases, the bacteria can also resists antibiotic drug's that doctors perscribe (such as amoxycillin) to fight infections. Bacterial rezistanse to such drugs has increase in recent years. the residue left behind by antibacterial soap is largely, responsible.

- words that compare
- punctuation with quotation marks

WEDNESDAY   Week 7

Some experts say that "antibacterial soap should be banned" because "we cannot afford to allow more superbugs to develop." Other Experts counter this argument, suggesting that antibacterial soap does not *necessarily* (nesesarilly) harm us but does not help us, either. Still others *declare* (declair) that *children* (childrens) who grow up in sanitized household's end up with immune systems that *do* (due) not *function* (funktion) *well* (good) enough to fight off germs that the children encounter out side of *their* (they're) homes. If this soap doesn't help us and possibly *causes* (cause) us harm, why should we use it at all? Bacteria certainly pose a problem to our health, but there is a sensible, safe solution.

Error Summary

Capitalization	1
Language Usage	3
Punctuation:	
Apostrophe	2
Comma	2
Question Mark	1
Quotation Mark	4
Spelling	7

THURSDAY   Week 7

There *are* (is) alternative ways to eliminate bacteria without using *no* *antibacterial* (antebactireal) soap. It might surprise you, to learn that ordinary soap is just as effective. In addition, many natural antibacterial Agents, such as lemon juice, Bleach, and *such as* hydrogen peroxide, *remove* (removes) germs without leaving a residue. The bacteria will be less likely, then, to survive, *reproduce* (reprodoose) and generate superbugs. The *best* (goodest) solution to the superbug problem seems to be to use lemon juice or bleach to clean house hold surfaces, and to use *ordinary* (ordinery) soap for washing hands. It also helps to wash your hands *briskly* (brisk), *thoroughly* (thorough), and often.

Error Summary

Capitalization	2
Language Usage	6
Punctuation:	
Comma	2
Sentence Structure	1
Spelling	4

WEDNESDAY   Week 7

- quotation marks
- adverbs
- verbs

Some experts say that "antibacterial soap should be banned" because "we cannot afford to allow more superbugs to develop." Other Experts counter this argument, sugjesting that antibacterial soap does not nesesarilly harm us but does not help us, either. Still others declair that childrens who grow up in sanitized household's end up with immune systems that due not funktion good enough to fight off germs that the children encounter out side of they're homes. If this soap doesnt help us and possibly cause us harm, why should we use it at all. Bacteria certainly pose a problem to our health but there is a sensible safe solution.

THURSDAY   Week 7

- words that compare
- parallel structure
- double negatives
- adverbs

There is alternative ways to eliminate bacteria without using no antebactireal soap. It might surprise you, to learn that ordinary soap is just as effective. In addition, many natural antibacterial Agents, such as lemon juice, Bleach, and such as hydrogen peroxide, removes germs without leaving a residue. The bacteria will be less likely, then, to survive, reprodoose and generate superbugs. The goodest solution to the superbug problem seems to be to use lemon juice or bleach to clean house hold surfaces, and to use ordinery soap for washing hands. It also helps to wash your hands brisk, thorough, and often.

MONDAY   Week 8

The Riace Bronzes

Riace (ree-AH-chee) is a small town in Calabria, a Mountainous region of Southern Italy. On august 16 1972, Riace met fame when a vacationing roman made an amazing discovery while swimming off the coast nearby. The swimmer stefano mariottini was exloring *(exploring)* underwater when he sees *(saw)* a life-size arm poking up from the floor of the ionian sea. He knew right away what it was Mariottini reports *(reported)* his discovery to the athoritees *(authorities)* in Calabria. Four days later divers lifted two enormous statue's out of the sea. After the statues were cleaned the mystery surounding *(surrounding)* them surfaced.

Error Summary

Capitalization	8
Language Usage	2
Punctuation:	
Apostrophe	1
Comma	5
Period	1
Spelling	3

TUESDAY   Week 8

The statues turned out to be from ancient greek times How did they end up buried in the sandy seafloor near Italy? Perhaps seafarers tossed they overbored *(them overboard)* to lighten a ships load during a storm This certainly would've lightened the load, because each statue weighs about 550 pounds (250 kilograms) Another explenation *(explanation)* is a ship wreck. Excavations of the area where mariottini found the statues revealed the keel of a old *(an)* Roman ship however, there isnt no *(any)* evidence to connect this ship to the statues. Still, it is possible that thiefs *(thieves)* took the statues during the roman occupation of greece And were on their way to rome when them *(they)* lost the treasure.

Error Summary

Capitalization	7
Language Usage	4
Punctuation:	
Apostrophe	3
Parentheses	1
Period	4
Question Mark	1
Spelling	4

Name _____

The Riace Bronzes

Riace (ree-AH-chee) is a small town in Calabria, a Mountainous region of Southern Italy. On august 16 1972, Riace met fame when a vacationing roman made an amazing discovery while swimming off the coast nearby. The swimmer stefano mariottini was exloring underwater when he sees a life-size arm poking up from the floor of the ionian sea. He knew right away what it was Mariottini reports his discovery to the athoritees in Calabria. Four days later divers lifted two enormous statue's out of the sea. After the statues were cleaned the mystery surounding them surfaced.

- personal names
- place names

The statues turned out to be from ancient greek times How did they end up buried in the sandy seafloor near Italy. Perhaps seafarers tossed they overbored to lighten a ships load during a storm This certainly wouldve lightened the load, because each statue weighs about 550 pounds (250 kilograms. Another explenation is a ship wreck. Excavations of the area where mariottini found the statues revealed the keel of a old Roman ship however, there isnt no evidence to connect this ship to the statues. Still, it is possible that thiefs took the statues during the roman occupation of greece. And were on their way to rome when them lost the treasure.

- pronouns
- apostrophes
- double negatives

WEDNESDAY   Week 8

The statues themselves are as ~~remarkible~~ [remarkable] as the mystery behind their location. But first, 2,000 year's worth of crusty sea formations had to be removed before the artistry of the statues ~~were visable~~ [was visible]. Its a time-consuming laborious process to remove such extensive ~~dibree~~ [debris]. Of major concern is preserving the statues ~~thru-out~~ [throughout] the process.

Once revealed, everyone recognized that the figures had been finely crafted. The two statues are in the form of men (ancient ~~greek~~ [greek] ~~wariors~~ [warriors]) and are ~~quiet~~ [quite] similar, with eyes made of ivory and glass, teeth of silver and lips of copper. ~~They're~~ [Their] age and craftsmanship ~~makes~~ [make] the statues rare.

Error Summary

Capitalization	3
Language Usage	2
Punctuation:	
Apostrophe	2
Comma	3
Hyphen	1
Parentheses	1
Sentence Structure	1
Spelling	7

THURSDAY   Week 8

One reason the statues are so valuable ~~are~~ [is] that few Greek bronzes survived from ancient times. The material was often melted down and reused to make ~~waepons~~ [weapons]. Some bronze's suffered from corrosion however the thick mud on the seafloor had ~~protect~~ [protected] the ~~riace~~ [riace] bronzes from either of these fates. The ~~impresive~~ [impressive] statues were exhibited in ~~florence~~ [florence] and ~~rome~~ [rome] in the early 1980s. Today, they are on display in the temperature-controlled basement of the National ~~museum~~ [museum] of ~~reggio calabria~~ [reggio calabria]. To protect them in this earthquake-prone region, the bronzes have been placed on ~~speshul~~ [special] supports to cushion against strong shaking movements.

Error Summary

Capitalization	7
Language Usage	2
Punctuation:	
Apostrophe	1
Comma	2
Hyphen	2
Period	1
Spelling	3

WEDNESDAY   Week 8

- verbs
- hyphens
- misplaced modifiers

The statues themselves are as remarkible as the mystery behind their location. But first, 2,000 year's worth of crusty sea formations had to be removed before the artistry of the statues were visable. Its a time consuming laborious process to remove such extensive dibree. Of major concern is preserving the statues thru-out the process.

Once revealed, everyone recognized that the figures had been finely crafted. The two statues are in the form of men (ancient greek wariors and are quiet similar, with eyes made of ivory and glass, teeth of silver and lips of copper. They're age and craftsmanship makes the statues rare.

THURSDAY   Week 8

- verbs
- hyphens
- place names
- names of buildings

One reason the statues are so valuable are that few Greek bronzes survived from ancient times. The material was often melted down and reused to make waepons. Some bronze's suffered from corrosion, however the thick mud on the seafloor had protect the riace bronzes, from either of these fates. The impresive statues were exhibited in florence and rome in the early 1980s. Today, they are on display in the temperature controlled basement of the National museum of reggio calabria. To protect them in this earthquake prone region, the bronzes have been placed on speshul supports to cushion against strong shaking movements.

MONDAY   Week 9

Ace Reporter Bly

Elizabeth Cochran was always ~~independant~~ *independent* some even called her rebellious. She left home as a 15-year-old so she could help support her widowed mother. The family had ~~fell~~ *fallen* into ~~pahverty~~ *poverty* still, it was difficult in the 1880s for women to find paid work. One day, Elizabeth read an article ~~entittled~~ *entitled* "What Girls Are Good For" in the Pittsburgh Dispatch a local newspaper. The article was written by Pittsburgh's most popular columnist. He said that ~~woman~~ *women* belonged at home cooking sewing and ~~to raise~~ *raising* children. A woman who worked away from home, he claimed, was a "monstrosity." Elizabeth was ~~furyus~~ *furious*.

Error Summary

Capitalization	2
Language Usage	2
Punctuation:	
Apostrophe	1
Comma	3
Hyphen	2
Period	2
Quotation Mark	3
Underlined Words	2
Sentence Structure	1
Spelling	4

TUESDAY   Week 9

Elizabeth wrote to the newspaper's editor and voiced her anger. She told him that the ~~news paper~~ *newspaper* should publish true realistic stories about the lives of ~~ordenarry~~ *ordinary* people. The ~~Editor george madden~~ *Editor George Madden*, was so ~~imprest~~ *impressed* with her passion and honesty that he ~~gived~~ *gave* her a writing ~~asignmint~~ *assignment*. He let her use the pen name by which she became known: Nellie Bly.

Nellie felt ~~strong~~ *strongly* about important social issues, and she was ~~a~~ *an* exceptional writer, too. She took her first writing opportunity to ~~enliten~~ *enlighten* readers about the struggles that poor working girls faced at the time. Madden knew he had to ~~hired~~ *hire* her as a full-time reporter.

Error Summary

Capitalization	3
Language Usage	4
Punctuation:	
Apostrophe	1
Colon	1
Comma	2
Hyphen	1
Period	2
Spelling	5

MONDAY   Week 9

Ace Reporter Bly

Elizabeth Cochran was always independant, some even called her rebellious. She left home as a 15 year old so she could help support her widowed mother. The family had fell into pahverty still, it was difficult in the 1880s for women to find paid work. One day, Elizabeth read an article entittled What Girls Are Good For in the Pittsburgh Dispatch a local newspaper. The article was written by Pittsburghs most popular columnist. He said that woman belonged at home cooking sewing and to raise children. A woman who worked away from home, he claimed, was a "monstrosity. Elizabeth was furyus.

WATCH FOR

- article titles
- names of newspapers
- parallel structure
- special words in quotation marks

TUESDAY   Week 9

Elizabeth wrote to the newspapers editor and voiced her anger. She told him that the news paper should publish true realistic stories about the lives of ordenarry people The Editor george madden, was so imprest with her passion and honesty that he gived her a writing asignmint. He let her use the pen name by which she became known Nellie Bly.

Nellie felt strong about important social issues, and she was a exceptional writer, too. She took her first writing opportunity to enliten readers about the struggles that poor working girls faced at the time. Madden knew he had to hired her as a full time reporter

WATCH FOR

- personal names
- colons
- adverbs

WEDNESDAY   Week 9

investigate
Nellie went on to ~~investtagate~~ child labor, low pay and
unsafe working conditions in a Pittsburgh Factory. Her work
write
finally reached joseph pulitzer who hired her to ~~writing~~ for
his newspaper, the New York World. Nellie often went
undercover in search of the truth. Once, she wrote about
conditions
the living ~~condishuns~~ for patients at new yorks home for
mentally ill patient's. There, nellie pretended to be ill
just so she could be admitted and she saw firsthand how
patients were   staff
the ~~patience was~~ treated by the ~~staf~~. The article she wrote
embarrassed
~~embarassed~~ New York city officials and prompted a change.
improved   institution
They soon ~~improves~~ the conditions in that ~~instatution~~.

Error Summary

Capitalization	7
Language Usage	3
Punctuation:	
Apostrophe	2
Comma	3
Underlined Words	3
Spelling	6

THURSDAY   Week 9

adventure
Nellie blys most famous ~~aventure~~ began in 1889.
Inspired by the 1873 novel by jules verne Around The world
proposed
in 80 days, she ~~proppozed~~ to do the same trip as phileas
Fogg (the book's fictional character). The trip would gain
publicity
~~publissity~~ for Pulitzers newspaper. Nellies goal was to travel
than
around the world faster ~~then~~ Phileas. Traveling alone by
carried
train, burro, and ship, Nellie ~~carryed~~ just one small suit case.
soared
Newspaper sales ~~sored~~ as people all over the country tracked
her travel's. She returned to New York in 72 days 6 hours
11 minutes, and 14 seconds—a record time in those days.
beaten   than
She had ~~beat~~ Phileas foggs time by more ~~then~~ a week.

Error Summary

Capitalization	8
Language Usage	3
Punctuation:	
Apostrophe	5
Comma	3
Parentheses	1
Underlined Words	6
Spelling	6

WEDNESDAY   Week 9

- names of newspapers
- place names
- apostrophes

Nellie went on to investtagate child labor, low pay and unsafe working conditions in a Pittsburgh Factory. Her work finally reached joseph pulitzer who hired her to writing for his newspaper, the New York World. Nellie often went undercover in search of the truth. Once, she wrote about the living condishuns for patients at new yorks home for mentally ill patient's. There, nellie pretended to be ill just so she could be admitted and she saw firsthand how the patience was treated by the staf. The article she wrote embarassed New York city officials and prompted a change. They soon improves the conditions in that instatution.

THURSDAY   Week 9

- book titles
- personal names
- punctuation with parentheses
- verbs

Nellie blys most famous aventure began in 1889. Inspired by the 1873 novel by jules verne Around The world in 80 days, she proppozed to do the same trip as phileas Fogg (the book's fictional character. The trip would gain publissity for Pulitzers newspaper. Nellies goal was to travel around the world faster then Phileas. Traveling alone by train, burro, and ship, Nellie carried just one small suit case. Newspaper sales sored as people all over the country tracked her travel's. She returned to New York in 72 days 6 hours 11 minutes, and 14 seconds—a record time in those days. She had beat Phileas foggs time by more then a week.

MONDAY   Week 10

Error Summary

Capitalization	6
Language Usage	1
Punctuation:	
Comma	7
Period	1
Underlined Words	2
Spelling	7

The Lake Michigan Triangle

People who like ~~storys~~ *stories* about paranormal ~~occurances~~ *occurrences* UFOs and unexplained ~~disapearinces~~ *disappearances*, may be intrigued by tales of the Lake Michigan Triangle. Strange events ~~their~~ *there* have been ~~document~~ *documented* for several decades. In her book entitled Weird Michigan and published in 2006, linda S godfrey describes this ~~trianguler~~ *triangular* region of central lake michigan. The towns of Ludington and Benton Harbor Michigan form two points of the triangle. manitowoc wisconsin is the third point. The things that happen in this region are so ~~astownding~~ *astounding* and ~~puzzeling~~ *puzzling* that people actually try to avoid the area.

TUESDAY   Week 10

Error Summary

Capitalization	4
Language Usage	6
Punctuation:	
Apostrophe	2
Comma	3
Period	1
Underlined Words	4
Spelling	4

The mysterious stories about this area started in 1891, when a ship named the thomas Hume disappeared. The ship and it's crew of seven men ~~was~~ *were* never found, even after an ~~extinsive~~ *extensive* search that didnt recover ~~nothing~~ *anything*. Another ~~wierd~~ *weird* event occurred in 1921, when a ship called the rosa belle was found floating in the lake, hull side up. It looked as if the ship ~~has~~ *had* been in a ~~colizhun~~ *collision* but no other ship had reported ~~no~~ *a* problem, there had been eleven people on board the ship but not a single trace of them ~~were~~ *was* found. The ~~bizarrest~~ *most bizarre* thing was that the Rosa Belle had experienced a ~~similiar~~ *similar* wreck in 1875, and was rebuilt after that event.

Name _____

• book titles
• place names

The Lake Michigan Triangle

People who like storys about paranormal occurances UFOs and unexplained disapearinces, may be intrigued by tales of the Lake Michigan Triangle. Strange events their have been document for several decades. In her book entitled Weird Michigan and published in 2006, linda S godfrey describes this trianguler region of central lake michigan. The towns of Ludington and Benton Harbor Michigan form two points of the triangle. manitowoc wisconsin is the third point. The things that happen in this region are so astownding and puzzeling that people actually try to avoid the area.

• names of ships
• double negatives
• words that compare

The mysterious stories about this area started in 1891, when a ship named the thomas Hume disappeared. The ship and it's crew of seven men was never found, even after an extinsive search that didnt recover nothing. Another wierd event occurred in 1921, when a ship called the rosa belle was found floating in the lake, hull side up. It looked as if the ship has been in a colizhun but no other ship had reported no problem, there had been eleven people on board the ship but not a single trace of them were found. The bizarrest thing was that the Rosa Belle had experienced a similiar wreck in 1875, and was rebuilt after that event.

WEDNESDAY   Week 10

Another ~~bizzare~~ *bizarre* event was reported in the <u>Cleveland Press</u> on april 29 1937. Apparently, the captain of a great lakes freighter called the <u>O.S. McFarland</u> disappeared on the night of April 28. He had just ~~pick~~ *picked* up 9,800 tons of coal from erie pennsylvania, and was headed for port washington wisconsin. The captain went to his cabin to take a nap after requesting that his crew awaken him when the ship neared port. Three hours later, the second mate found the captains' cabin empty the entire crew ~~search~~ *searched* the ship ~~thorough~~ *thoroughly* but the captain was never found. One odd but important detail is that his cabin door was locked from the in side.

Error Summary

Capitalization	11
Language Usage	3
Punctuation:	
Apostrophe	1
Comma	4
Period	1
Underlined Words	4
Spelling	2

THURSDAY   Week 10

The legend of the triangle ~~apply~~ *applies* to aircraft, too. On june 23 1950 a northwest airlines plane with 58 people on board left new york city, headed for minneapolis. The last radio contact with the aircraft conveyed that it was changing it's course and would be flying over Lake michigan because of bad ~~whether~~ *weather*; it never arrived at its destination. ~~Fragmints~~ *Fragments* of bodies and ~~debrie was~~ *debris were* found floating on the lake's surface but diver's never located the ~~wreckege~~ *wreckage* of the plane. Neither this ~~or~~ *nor* other ~~unforchunate~~ *unfortunate* events occurring within the Lake Michigan Triangle ~~has~~ *have* ever been proven to be of supernatural origins but they are undeniably ~~all~~ strange

Error Summary

Capitalization	9
Language Usage	4
Punctuation:	
Apostrophe	2
Comma	4
Period	1
Sentence Structure	1
Spelling	5

WEDNESDAY   Week 10

Another bizzare event was reported in the Cleveland Press on april 29 1937. Apparently, the captain of a great lakes freighter called the O.S. McFarland disappeared on the night of April 28. He had just pick up 9,800 tons of coal from erie pennsylvania, and was headed for port washington wisconsin. The Captain went to his cabin to take a nap after requesting that his crew awaken him when the ship neared Port. Three hours later, the second mate found the captains' cabin empty the entire crew search the ship thorough but the captain was never found. One odd but important detail is that his cabin door was locked from the in side.

WATCH FOR

- names of newspapers
- place names
- dates
- verbs

THURSDAY   Week 10

The legend of the triangle apply to aircraft, too. On june 23 1950 a northwest airlines plane with 58 people on board left new york city, headed for minneapolis. The last radio contact with the aircraft conveyed that it was changing it's course and would be flying over Lake michigan because of bad whether; it never arrived at its destination. Fragmints of bodies and debrie was found floating on the lake's surface but diver's never located the wreckege of the plane. Neither this or other unforchunate events occurring within the Lake Michigan Triangle has ever been proven to be of Supernatural origins but they are undeniably all strange

WATCH FOR

- company names
- verbs
- dates
- misplaced modifiers

MONDAY — Week 11

Error Summary
Capitalization	3
Language Usage	2
Punctuation:	
Apostrophe	3
Comma	9
Period	1
Spelling	8

The Hornbek Homestead

Most of us do not ~~reflekt~~ reflect often on what it ~~take~~ takes to build the homes we live in. Families' in the 1800s (especially Pioneers who built homes on the western frontier) however had to consider such things. Adeline hornbek a pioneer and widowed mother, was recognized as having ~~a~~ an out standing home stead. It was special Because it was innovative for it's time. Even today the setting is note worthy. Adeline ~~purchised~~ purchased 160 ~~acers~~ acres of open land in Colorados Florissant Valley in 1878. The fertile valley with grassy meadows and wildflowers in spring wears a far away crown of ~~mountan~~ mountain peaks.

TUESDAY — Week 11

Error Summary
Capitalization	6
Punctuation:	
Apostrophe	3
Comma	6
Hyphen	3
Parentheses	1
Period	2
Spelling	4

The size of the hornbek homestead was one thing that set it apart from other's on the ~~fronteer~~ frontier a one-room house was typical for most pioneers. Adelines two-story house had four bedrooms, a parlor and a ~~kichen~~ kitchen. It also had nine outbuildings. (an outbuilding is part of the property but not connected to it.) The outbuildings included a log house, a chicken house a milk house and stables. The main house had a dozen glass-paned windows. It was the first multistory house to be built in the florissant Valley. During Adelines time, the house had fancy ~~furnashings~~ furnishings Which contrasted with the ~~rustick~~ rustic setting of the ranch

Name _____

MONDAY   Week 11

The Hornbek Homestead

Most of us do not reflekt often on what it take to build the homes we live in. Families' in the 1800s, (especially Pioneers who built homes on the western frontier) however had to consider such things. Adeline hornbek a pioneer and widowed mother, was recognized as having a out standing home stead. It was special. Because it was innovative for it's time. Even today the setting is, note worthy. Adeline purchased 160 acers of open land in Colorados Florissant Valley in 1878. The fertile valley with grassy meadows, and wildflowers in spring wears a far away crown of mountan peaks.

- commas
- incomplete sentences
- compound words

TUESDAY   Week 11

The size of the hornbek homestead was one thing that set it apart from other's on the fronteer, a one room house was typical for most pioneers. Adelines' two story house had four bedrooms, a parlor and a kichen. It also had nine outbuildings. (an outbuilding is part of the property but not connected to it). The outbuildings included a log house, a chicken house a milk house and, stables. The main house had a dozen, glass paned windows. It was the first multistory house to be built in the florissant Valley. During Adelines time, the house had fancy furnashings. Which contrasted with the rustick setting of the ranch

- names of buildings
- hyphens
- commas
- punctuation with parentheses

WEDNESDAY   Week 11

The location of Adeline's homestead was high [highly]
advantageous for a ranch. it is unlikely that adeline chose
this location by accident, because she was a [an] intelligent
resoursfull [resourceful] woman The Homestead was situated along a
tributary or small branch of the South platte River which
provided conveenyent [convenient] access to water. In edition [addition], the river's
proximity allowed Adeline to transport goods into the area.
And to ship agricultural products to market. The soil was
fertile and livestalk [livestock] could graze free [freely] in the broad open
meadows. Nearby forests of ponderosa pine Provided the
timber for constructing buildings and fences.

Error Summary

Capitalization	6
Language Usage	4
Punctuation:	
Apostrophe	1
Comma	6
Period	3
Spelling	3

THURSDAY   Week 11

Adelines [Adeline's] log house still stand [stands] today the uninhabited
homestead is a tiny ghost town on a friendly oddly welcoming
field. The US Government mainetanes [maintains] and preserves the
homestead which is now part of a National Park. Some of
the original outbuilding's [outbuildings] no longer remains [remain]. In fact the
National park service has moved buildings from similar
properties in the vassinity [vicinity] (houses from other homesteads)
onto the Hornbek Homestead land to give the appearance of
the Original outbuildings that use [used] to be there. Dispite [Despite] the
changes, the Hornbek property still represents innovation in
Pioneer housing of the 1800s.

Error Summary

Capitalization	8
Language Usage	3
Punctuation:	
Apostrophe	2
Comma	3
Parentheses	1
Period	3
Spelling	3

Name _____

WEDNESDAY   Week 11

The location of Adeline's homestead was high advantageous for a ranch. it is unlikely that adeline chose this location by accident, because she was a intelligent resoursfull woman The Homestead was situated along a tributary or small branch of the South platte River which provided conveenyent access to water. In edition, the rivers proximity allowed Adeline to transport goods into the area. And to ship agricultural products to market. The soil was fertile and livestalk could graze free in the broad open meadows. Nearby forests of ponderosa pine. Provided the timber for constructing buildings and fences.

- adverbs
- commas
- incomplete sentences

THURSDAY   Week 11

Adelines log house still stand today, the uninhabited homestead is a tiny ghost town on a friendly oddly welcoming field. The US Government mainetanes and preserves the homestead which is now part of a National Park. Some of the original outbuilding's no longer remains. In fact the National park service has moved buildings from similar properties in the vassinity (houses from other homesteads onto the Hornbek Homestead land to give the appearance of the Original outbuildings that use to be there. Dispite the changes, the Hornbek property still represents innovation in Pioneer housing of the 1800s.

- run-on sentences
- abbreviations
- parentheses
- names of organizations

MONDAY   Week 12

Error Summary

Capitalization	9
Language Usage	3
Punctuation:	
Comma	8
Quotation Mark	1
Spelling	4

The Wind Tamer

My name is william Kamkwamba, and I was born on august 5, 1987, in Malawi africa. My village masitala, is in the most fertile *district* in all of malawi. People often call this part of the country the "breadbasket." It used to be easy to grow crops on our small farms. Seeds were cheap, and president Hastings Banda made sure that every farming family had *fertilizer*. As long as the rain fell, every one *had* plenty to eat. In 1994, though, farming became more difficult, because the policies of our new leader, Bakili muluzi *were* not as *helpful* to Farmers as *those* of our former President.

TUESDAY   Week 12

Error Summary

Capitalization	4
Language Usage	3
Punctuation:	
Apostrophe	2
Comma	4
Hyphen	1
Period	1
Spelling	7

President Muluzi *halted* all government aid to farmers. Without any money to hire workers, Families had to do all the work them selves. That's why, at the age of seven, I was already a hard-working farmer. But I also went to school. And learned about science and other things.

December of 2000 was the beginning of disaster for my country. The rains *were* late. Then they were *too* heavy. Floods *carried* away any Seedlings that *had* started to grow. After that, we had a terrible *drought*. It didn't take long for food to *become* so *scarce*, that people were dying of starvation. Then an *epidemic* of cholera swept the Country.

MONDAY   Week 12

The Wind Tamer

My name is william Kamkwamba, and I was born on august 5 1987, in Malawi africa. My village masitala, is in the most fertile distrikt in all of malawi. People often call this part of the country the "breadbasket. It used to be easy to grow crops on our small farms. Seeds were cheap and president Hastings Banda made sure that every farming family had furtellizer. As long as the rain fell every one have plenty to eat. In 1994 though farming became more difficult, because the policies of our new leader, Bakili muluzi was not as helpfull to Farmers as that of our former President.

- dates
- special words in quotation marks
- titles of people

TUESDAY   Week 12

President Muluzi haulted all government aid to farmers. Without any money to hire workers. Families had to do all the work them selves. Thats why, at the age of seven, I was already a hard working farmer. But I also went to school. And learned about science and other things.

December of 2000, was the beginning of disaster for my country. The rains was late. Then they were to heavy. Floods carryed away any Seedlings that have started to grow. After that, we had a terrible drowt. It didnt take long for food to became so skars, that people were dying of starvation. Then an epidemmic, of cholera swept the Country.

- incomplete sentences
- verbs
- hyphens

WEDNESDAY　　　　　　　　　　　　　　　Week 12

      I ~~stop~~ stopped going to school, because my family ~~could'nt~~ couldn't afford the ~~tooishun~~ tuition. I ~~begun~~ began using a local library that ~~were~~ was ~~stalked~~ stocked with books donated by the U.S. ~~governmant~~ government. I read about many things that interested me, such as Magnetism and Electricity. One day, ~~quiet~~ quite by accident, I came across a textbook entitled <u>Using energy</u>. that book which was about windmills, ~~changes~~ changed my life. As I read it, I realized that a windmill, would immensely improve the lives of everyone in my village. It would ~~gennerrate~~ generate enough power so we could have electricity at home, and would allow us to pump water from an a well to irrigate a year-round garden.

Error Summary

Capitalization	4
Language Usage	5
Punctuation:	
Comma	3
Hyphen	1
Underlined Words	2
Spelling	6

THURSDAY　　　　　　　　　　　　　　　Week 12

      I decided to build a windmill near my house. I was Hopeful that we would have ~~elektrisity~~ electricity then we would be able to stay up after the Sun went down. After much trial and error, I finally assembled a windmill that worked. I used wood from local ~~tree's~~ trees, bicycle ~~part's~~ parts and various other materials that I'd found in the local scrapyard. People from my village and from ~~naybering~~ neighboring villages ~~was ellated~~ were elated when the windmill gave us enough power to light a single bulb! It was a ~~moddest~~ modest start, we soon had more lights. And were able to pump water. Since then, people have ~~call~~ called me a hero. I don't think that's true, I just saw a problem, and tried to fix it.

Error Summary

Capitalization	5
Language Usage	2
Punctuation:	
Apostrophe	5
Comma	3
Period	4
Spelling	4

WEDNESDAY   Week 12

I stop going to school, because my family could'nt afford the tooishun. I begun using a local library that were stalked with books donated by the U.S. governmant. I read about many things that interested me, such as Magnetism and Electricity. One day, quiet by accident, I came across a textbook entitled Using energy. that book which was about windmills, changes my life. As I read it, I realized that a windmill, would immensely improve the lives of everyone in my village. It would gennerrate enough power so we could have electricity at home, and would allow us to pump water from an well to irrigate a year round garden.

- verbs
- book titles
- hyphens

THURSDAY   Week 12

I decided to build a windmill near my house. I was Hopeful that we would have elektrisity then we would be able to stay up after the Sun went down. After much trial and error I finally assembled a windmill that worked. I used wood from local tree's, bicycle part's and various other materials that Id found in the local scrapyard. People from my village and from nayboring villages was ellated when the windmill gave us enough power to light a single bulb! It was a moddest start, we soon had more lights. And were able to pump water. Since then, people have call me a hero. I dont think thats true, I just saw a problem, and tried to fix it.

- run-on sentences
- apostrophes

MONDAY   Week 13

Saving Our Heritage

Cahokia Mounds, located near St louis Missouri is the site of a thriving city that was inhabited centuries before Columbuss ~~arival~~ arrival on the continent. The ruins, designated by UNESCO as ~~an~~ a world heritage site in 1982, are preserved and protected so ~~visiters~~ visitors can learn about how pre-Columbian people lived in north america. Cahokia is only one of more ~~then~~ than 900 world heritage ~~sights~~ sites. Funding these properties ~~cost~~ costs a small fortune and some people think it isnt worth it. however I believe that its ~~esential~~ essential to protect sites such as cahokia mounds so they wont be lost forever.

Error Summary
Capitalization	6
Language Usage	3
Punctuation:	
Apostrophe	4
Comma	4
Period	1
Spelling	4

TUESDAY   Week 13

When we study old cultures we learn how people ~~addapt~~ adapt to their ~~environment~~ environment and cope with natural disasters. We learn how patterns of migration ~~affects~~ affect languages and why civilizations thrive or die out. Studying the ~~remnints~~ remnants of culture ~~help~~ helps us understand how people lived long ago, and helps us understand our own ~~civilazation~~ civilization. However not all of the world heritage sites are ancient ruins also included are australias modern Sydney Opera House, the tower of london in england, the statue of liberty in New York Harbor, and other recognizable structures. These are all ~~impresive~~ impressive places of outstanding value to people around the world.

Error Summary
Capitalization	7
Language Usage	2
Punctuation:	
Apostrophe	1
Comma	3
Period	1
Spelling	5

MONDAY   Week 13

- abbreviations
- place names
- verbs

Saving Our Heritage

Cahokia Mounds, located near St louis Missouri is the site of a thriving city that was inhabited centuries before Columbuss arival on the continent. The ruins, designated by UNESCO as an world heritage site in 1982, are preserved and protected so visiters can learn about how pre-Columbian people lived in north america. Cahokia is only one of more then 900 world heritage sights. Funding these properties cost a small fortune and some people think it isnt worth it. however I believe that its esential to protect sites such as cahokia mounds so they wont be lost forever.

TUESDAY   Week 13

- run-on sentences
- place names
- names of buildings

When we study old cultures we learn how people addapt to their envirenment and cope with natural disasters. We learn how patterns of migration affects languages and why civilizations thrive or die out. Studying the remnints of culture help us understand how people lived long ago, and helps us understand our own civilazation. However not all of the world heritage sites are ancient ruins, also included are australias modern Sydney Opera House, the tower of london in england, the statue of liberty in New York Harbor, and other recognizable structures. These are all impresive places of outstanding value to people around the world.

WEDNESDAY   Week 13

Some people may ~~wander~~ wonder why places like the Tower of ~~london~~ need preservation. The simple answer is that all structures need ~~maintenence~~ maintenance they fall apart otherwise. Forces such as earthquakes, floods, and windstorms threaten heritage properties, so ~~does~~ do war and poverty. People can't always afford to protect the historic buildings near them, which is why Unesco helps. Imagine if the great places of the world—famous Cathedrals and Temples, Palaces, Castles, Caves with prehistoric paintings, and statues carved into the sides of mountains—~~was~~ were all ~~dstroyed~~ destroyed. They are important to everyone in the world, not just to the people ~~whom~~ who live near them.

Error Summary

Capitalization	13
Language Usage	3
Punctuation:	
Comma	5
Period	3
Spelling	3

THURSDAY   Week 13

~~Opponints~~ Opponents of unesco ~~believes~~ believe that the organization ~~have~~ has no business interfering with property in ~~soveriegn~~ sovereign countries. They think local ~~resedents~~ residents or ~~goverments~~ governments should do whatever they want with properties on their own soil. Or be solely responsible for ~~preserveing~~ preserving properties. I don't agree. Suppose developers decided to tear down the great wall of china or construct private homes at machu picchu in peru. These sites have ~~universel~~ universal importance, everyone should be able to visit these places if they can. As world heritage sites, I am glad to know that these treasured places can be protected for future generations.

Error Summary

Capitalization	15
Language Usage	2
Punctuation:	
Period	3
Sentence Structure	1
Spelling	6

WEDNESDAY   Week 13

- end punctuation
- run-on sentences
- acronyms
- pronouns

Some people may wander why places like the Tower of london, need preservation? The simple answer is that all structures need maintenence, they fall apart otherwise. Forces such as earthquakes floods and windstorms threaten heritage properties, so does war and poverty. People can't always afford to protect the historic buildings near them which is why Unesco helps. Imagine if the great places of the world—famous Cathedrals and Temples, Palaces, Castles, Caves with prehistoric paintings, and statues carved into the sides of mountains—was all dstroyed. They are important to everyone in the world not just to the people whom live near them.

THURSDAY   Week 13

- acronyms
- misplaced modifiers

Opponints of unesco believes that the organization have no business interfering with property in soveriegn countries. They think local resedents or goverments should do whatever they want with properties on their own soil. Or be solely responsible for preserveing properties. I don't agree. Suppose developers decided to tear down the great wall of china or construct private homes at machu picchu in peru? These sites have universel importance, everyone should be able to visit these places if they can. As world heritage sites, I am glad to know that these treasured places, can be protected for future generations.

MONDAY   Week 14

Old Stormalong

If you've never heard of alfred bulltop stormalong from massachusetts, this story will be a treat. He's usually called "Old Stormalong," but he *wasn't* always old. He started out young—just like everyone else. But that's the only thing about Old Stormalong that was *ordinary*. For one thing, he *was* enormous as a newborn baby; not many years later, he was five fathoms tall. (That's a sailor's way of saying thirty feet, give or take a foot.) One day, when he was still a youngster, he strolled down to the docks whistling "The Rambling Sailor," while looking for a job; he was employed almost *immediately*.

Error Summary
Capitalization	6
Language Usage	1
Punctuation:	
Apostrophe	5
Comma	4
Parentheses	1
Period	2
Quotation Mark	3
Spelling	3

TUESDAY   Week 14

Now, you might be *asking* yourself, "What could such a young lad do on a ship?" Well, he was about the *most perfect* person to stand watch! The Captain realized right away that this boy would be able to see *farther* than anyone else because of his *tremendous* size. He wouldn't even *have* to use the crow's nest to get a good view. (A crow's nest is a platform attached to the *tallest* mast of a ship. From that position, a lookout can see land, ship's, or *hazards* at a distance.) Once the *captain* hired Old Stormalong (well, he was Young Stormalong in those days), that crow's nest didn't get *any* more use. Stormalong was made for a sailor's life.

Error Summary
Capitalization	1
Language Usage	6
Punctuation:	
Apostrophe	4
Comma	3
Parentheses	2
Period	1
Quotation Mark	1
Spelling	4

MONDAY   **Week 14**

Old Stormalong

If youve never heard of alfred bulltop stormalong from massachusetts, this story will be a treat. Hes usually called "Old Stormalong but he was'nt always old. He started out young—just like everyone else. But thats the only thing about Old Stormalong that was ordinery. For one thing he were enormous as a newborn baby, not many years later he was five fathoms tall. (Thats a sailors way of saying thirty feet, give or take a foot. One day, when he was still a youngster he strolled down to the docks whistling The Rambling Sailor while looking for a job he was employed almost imediateley.

- personal names
- special words in quotation marks
- parentheses
- run-on sentences
- song titles

TUESDAY   **Week 14**

Now, you might be ask yourself, "What could such a young lad do on a ship"? Well he was about the perfectest person to stand watch! The Captain realized right away that this boy would be able to see farthest than anyone else because of his trimmendus size. He wouldnt even has to use the crow's nest to get a good view. (A crows nest is a plat form attached to the most tall mast of a ship. From that position, a lookout can see land ship's or hazerds at a distance). Once the captin hired Old Stormalong (well, he was Young Stormalong in those days, that crow's nest didn't get no more use. Stormalong was made for a sailors life

- commas
- punctuation with quotation marks
- words that compare
- punctuation with parentheses

WEDNESDAY   Week 14

Error Summary

Capitalization	4
Language Usage	2
Punctuation:	
Apostrophe	1
Comma	3
Period	2
Spelling	6

After a few years, stormalong began to feel that he
had ~~outgrew~~ (outgrown) the ship. He wanted a ship of his own, so he
~~commisioned~~ (commissioned) a shipwright to build one. He called it the
Courser. it was undoubtedly the largest ship ever ~~asembled~~ (assembled).
The deck was so long that the crew needed horses to travel
from stem to stern—in other words, from the front of the
ship to the back. The sail's were so ~~emence~~ (immense) that they had
to be ~~sown~~ (sewn) together in the ~~dessert~~ (desert) where the land was open
and flat enough to ~~strech~~ (stretch) out the sails. The mast was so
tall, that it had to be hinged in the middle, then it could
be ~~took~~ (taken) down to let the sun and the Moon pass by.

THURSDAY   Week 14

Error Summary

Capitalization	7
Language Usage	6
Punctuation:	
Apostrophe	4
Comma	1
Underlined Words	1
Spelling	8

The courser was so ~~collosul~~ (colossal) that no Harbor could hold
it. That's why it was always in deep water. Sailing ~~thorough~~ (through)
the english channel was quite an ~~ordeel~~ (ordeal). The crew didnt
~~never~~ (ever) want to repeat it. The ship was so wide that it got
~~stucked~~ (stuck) halfway. Stormalong had a (an) idea though. He ~~asks~~ (asked) the
crew to rub soap all over the ship's hull to make it ~~slippary~~ (slippery).
The ship barely ~~skweezed~~ (squeezed) through. To this day, the cliffs
near dover is (are) chalky white from all the soap that scraped off
the Courser. After that, the ~~rezaddents~~ (residents) along englands coast
asked Stormalong to avoid the Channel. But they phrased
~~they're~~ (their) request very ~~polite~~ (politely) so as not to ~~afend~~ (offend) him.

Name _____

WEDNESDAY	Week 14

- personal names
- verbs
- commas

After a few years, stormalong began to feel that he had outgrew the ship. He wanted a ship of his own so he commisioned a shipwright to build one. He called it the Courser it was undoubtedly the largest ship ever asembled. The deck was so long that the crew needed horses to travel from stem to stern—in other words, from the front of the ship to the back. The sail's were so emence that they had to be sown together in the dessert where the land was open and flat enough to strech out the sails. The mast was so tall, that it had to be hinged in the middle, then it could be took down to let the sun and the Moon pass by.

THURSDAY	Week 14

- names of ships
- place names
- double negatives

The courser was so collosul that no Harbor could hold it. Thats why it was always in deep water. Sailing thorough the english channel was quite an ordeel. The crew didnt never want to repeat it. The ship was so wide that it got stucked halfway. Stormalong had a idea though. He asks the crew to rub soap all over the ships hull to make it slippary. The ship barely skweezed through. To this day, the cliffs near dover is chalky white from all the soap that scraped off the Courser. After that, the rezaddents along englands coast asked Stormalong to avoid the Channel. But they phrased they're request very polite so as not to afend him.

MONDAY   Week 15

Error Summary

Capitalization	3
Language Usage	5
Punctuation:	
Apostrophe	1
Comma	2
Hyphen	3
Period	2
Quotation Mark	1
Spelling	3

The Legend Behind Spouting Horn

On the scenic south shore of the hawaiian island Kauai (kah-WAH-ee) lies a natural wonder called Spouting Horn. If you visits [visit] this spot which is a magnet for Tourists you may see salt water spurt 50 feet from a [an] opening in a cave-like rock formation below the sea. Nearby, a [an] eerie moaning noise emerge [emerges] from another opening in the "cave", but this one doesnt spray like a fountain. The tube-shaped formashun [formation] greetes [greets] each and every wave that crashes onto shore with a breathtaking gush of water and a [an] ominous sound the ancient leggend [legend] about Liko (LEE-koh) and mo'o (MOH-oh) explains it

TUESDAY   Week 15

Error Summary

Capitalization	6
Language Usage	4
Punctuation:	
Comma	2
Parentheses	1
Period	1
Spelling	5

A mo'o is a lizzerd [lizard]. In Hawaii, this reptile is regarded as a powerful gardian [guardian] spirit that protects house holds [households] and areas of land and water. She is also the focus of many hawaiian myths and legends, sometimes appearing as a dragon.

In the legend of spouting horn, the mo'o was of a monstrous size (nearly 30 feet long. She guard [guarded] the coast of kauai with a [an] ever-watchful eye, and was agresive [aggressive] toward anyone, who tried to tresspas [trespass]. Fisherman [Fishermen] and swimmers alike knew that it was unwise to visit the coast where the mo'o patrolled. However there was one unlucky person who had never hear [heard] about the mo'o. His name was Liko.

Name _____

The Legend Behind Spouting Horn

On the scenic south shore of the hawaiian island Kauai (kah-WAH-ee) lies a natural wonder called Spouting Horn. If you visits this spot which is a magnet for Tourists you may see salt water spurt 50 feet from a opening in a cave-like rock formation below the sea. Nearby, a eerie moaning noise emerge from another opening in the "cave", but this one doesnt spray like-a-fountain. The tube shaped formashun greetes each and every wave that crashes onto shore with a breathtaking gush of water and a ominous sound, the ancient leggend about Liko (LEE-koh) and mo'o (MOH-oh) explains it

- compound words
- punctuation with quotation marks
- hyphens

A mo'o is a lizzerd. In Hawaii, this reptile is regarded as a powerful gardian spirit that protects house holds and areas of land and water. She is also the focus of many hawaiian myths and legends, sometimes appearing as a dragon.

In the Legend of spouting horn, the mo'o was of a monstrous size (nearly 30 feet long. She guard the coast of kauai with a ever-watchful eye. And was agresive toward anyone, who tried to tresspas. Fisherman and swimmers alike knew that it was unwise to visit the coast where the mo'o patrolled. However there was one unlucky person who had never hear about the mo'o. His name was Liko.

- place names
- punctuation with parentheses
- incomplete sentences
- verbs

WEDNESDAY　　　　　　　　　　　　　　　Week 15

Poor Liko, not ~~reelizing~~ **realizing** that the moʻo could ~~devower~~ **devour** a person, chose to swim ~~direct~~ **directly** into the lizards **territory** ~~teratory~~. The moʻo saw Liko as an ~~introoder~~ **intruder**. Liko spotted the huge lizard swimming ~~vigorous~~ **vigorously** toward him, preparing to gobble him up. Liko held his breath ~~swum~~ **swam** below the waters surface and escaped the moʻo by squeezing into an underwater sea cave (We know this place as Spouting Horn today.) liko swam out of the caves other mouth, located on the rocky shore. The moʻo tried to follow Liko but she got stuck in the cave. Due to her imposing size. According to legend, the moʻo is still stuck in the cave, ~~groning~~ **groaning** with anger and hunger.

Error Summary

Capitalization	2
Language Usage	3
Punctuation:	
Apostrophe	3
Comma	3
Parentheses	1
Period	2
Spelling	5

THURSDAY　　　　　　　　　　　　　　　Week 15

The legend of spouting horn has some ~~varieties~~ **variations**. in one version, Liko ~~peerces~~ **pierces** the moʻo with a spear before the moʻo gets stuck and that's why the moʻo cries and moans in pain In another rendition, Liko intentionally challenges the moʻo rather than ~~stumbeling~~ **stumbling** on her territory ~~accidently~~ **accidentally**.

In reality, the ~~phenonemon~~ **phenomenon** of Spouting Horn is caused by ~~preshur~~ **pressure**. Oncoming waves push air and water into a hollow, underwater, rock formation known as a "lava tube." How did this tube form? Long ago, a stream of lava flowing into the ocean cooled quickly, the ~~perrimiter~~ **perimeter** hardened but the lava inside drained away. The result is Spouting Horn.

Error Summary

Capitalization	5
Punctuation:	
Comma	3
Period	2
Question Mark	1
Spelling	7

WEDNESDAY   Week 15

Poor Liko, not reelizing that the mo'o could devower a person, chose to swim direct into the lizards teratory. The mo'o saw Liko as an introoder. Liko spotted the huge lizard swimming vigorous toward him, preparing to gobble him up. Liko held his breath swum below the waters surface and escaped the mo'o by squeezing into an underwater sea cave (We know this place as Spouting Horn today. liko swam out of the caves other mouth, located on the rocky shore. The mo'o tried to follow Liko but she got stuck in the cave. Due to her imposing size. According to legend, the mo'o is still stuck in the cave, groning with anger and hunger.

- adverbs
- apostrophes
- parentheses

THURSDAY   Week 15

The legend of spouting horn has some varietions. in one version, Liko peerces the mo'o with a spear before the mo'o gets stuck and that's why the mo'o cries and moans in pain In another rendition, Liko intentionally challenges the mo'o rather than stumbeling on her territory accidently.

In reality, the phenonemon of Spouting Horn is caused by preshur. Oncoming waves push air and water into a hollow, underwater, rock formation known as a "lava tube." How did this tube form. Long ago, a stream of Lava flowing into the ocean cooled quickly, the perrimiter hardened but the lava inside drained away. The result is Spouting Horn.

- place names
- verbs
- run-on sentences

MONDAY   Week 16

The Tuskegee Airmen

A 2012 movie called <u>Red Tails</u> ~~tell~~ [tells] the story of the
Tuskegee Airmen. The first black pilots in the U.S. armed
forces. The movie title ~~refer~~ [refers] to the fact that these pilots
(mostly african americans) painted the tails of ~~they're plains~~ [their planes]
red. And were themselves nicknamed "Red Tails." These men
served with ~~braverie~~ [bravery] during world war II. Their primary job
was to escort, or guide, other planes on bombing missions,
and they protected those planes with their own lives. Despite
much ~~oposition~~ [opposition] to allowing black servicemen to become military
pilots. The contribution of these airmen was ~~perfound~~ [profound].

Error Summary

Capitalization	7
Language Usage	2
Punctuation:	
Apostrophe	1
Comma	3
Period	1
Quotation Mark	1
Underlined Words	2
Spelling	5

TUESDAY   Week 16

The story of the Tuskegee Airmen began in 1941. It's
important, though, to understand the conditions leading up to
the story. Until the 1940s, African Americans in the ~~milatery~~ [military]
were prevented from doing many jobs. They ~~could'nt~~ [couldn't] hold ~~no~~ [any]
positions of leadership, nor were they ~~purmited~~ [permitted] to take jobs
that required training. Furthermore, the armed forces were
segregated. Two ~~deccades~~ [decades] of Civil Rights ~~efferts~~ [efforts] finally ~~lead~~ [led]
congress to pass a bill in 1939. That set aside funds for
the training of African American ~~pillots~~ [pilots]. ~~Founded in 1881 by~~
~~Booker T. Washington,~~ the training program was established
at alabamas Tuskegee institute. [founded in 1881 by Booker T. Washington]

Error Summary

Capitalization	7
Language Usage	1
Punctuation:	
Apostrophe	2
Comma	3
Period	1
Sentence Structure	1
Spelling	7

Name _____

The Tuskegee Airmen

A 2012 movie called Red Tails tell the story of the Tuskegee Airmen. The first black pilots in the U.S. armed force's. The movie title refer to the fact that these pilots (mostly african americans) painted the tails of they're plains red. And were themselves nicknamed "Red Tails. These men served with braverie during world war II. Their primary job was to escort or guide, other planes on bombing missions, and they protected those planes with their own lives. Despite much oposition to allowing black servicemen to become military pilots. The contribution of these airmen was perfound.

WATCH FOR

- movie titles
- incomplete sentences
- historic events
- punctuation with quotation marks

The story of the Tuskegee Airmen began in 1941. Its important though to understand the conditions leading up to the story. Until the 1940s, African Americans in the milatery were prevented from doing many jobs. They could'nt hold no positions of Leadership, nor were they purmited to take jobs that required training. Furthermore the armed forces were segregated. Two deccades of Civil Rights efferts finally lead congress to pass a bill in 1939. That set aside funds for the training of African American pillots. Founded in 1881 by Booker T. Washington, the training program was established at alabamas Tuskegee institute.

WATCH FOR

- double negatives
- misplaced modifiers

WEDNESDAY   Week 16

Training for the tuskegee airmen were [was] not just for pilots. Rather it was for all the personnel needed to keep planes in the air This included pilots navigators bombardiers instructors, and fixing the planes mechanically [mechanics].

About five months after the flight program began First lady Eleanor Roosevelt arrived for a vissit [visit]. She flew as a passinjer [passenger] in a biplane (a small aircraft with two wings on each side) The pilot, who was a [an] instructor for the program, was C. alfred anderson but everyone called him "Chief." The 30-minute flight impressed mrs roosevelt. Afterword [Afterward], she kindly vowcht [vouched] for the pilot's skill.

Error Summary

Capitalization	7
Language Usage	2
Punctuation:	
Comma	6
Hyphen	1
Parentheses	1
Period	2
Quotation Mark	1
Sentence Structure	1
Spelling	4

THURSDAY   Week 16

The Tuskegee Airmen had a [an] impressive combat reckerd [record] during the War. In total, 992 pilots graduated and flew aircraft in more then [than] 1,578 war missions. In addition the men destroy [destroyed] 261 Enemy Aircraft. and was awerded [were awarded] 850 medals The group are [is] one of the most deckerated [decorated] units of the U.S. Army. Some pilots flyed [flew] as many as 100 missions—more than they were supposed to fly—because reinforsemints [reinforcements] for the all-black unit was [were] scarce. The pilots remain [remained] active until 1946, well after the war had ended. Aside from the fact that they served honoribly [honorably] they also paved the way for racial integration in the U.S. military.

Error Summary

Capitalization	3
Language Usage	8
Punctuation:	
Comma	3
Hyphen	1
Period	1
Spelling	5

WEDNESDAY   Week 16

Training for the tuskegee airmen were not just for pilots. Rather it was for all the personnel needed to keep planes in the air This included pilots navigators bombardiers instructors, and fixing the planes mechanically.

About five months after the flight program began First lady Eleanor Roosevelt arrived for a vissit. She flew as a passinjer in a biplane (a small aircraft with two wings on each side.) The pilot, who was a instructor for the program, was C. alfred anderson but everyone called him "Chief. The 30 minute flight impressed mrs roosevelt. Afterword, she kindly vowcht for the pilot's skill.

WATCH FOR

- parallel structure
- punctuation with parentheses
- titles of people
- hyphens

THURSDAY   Week 16

The Tuskegee Airmen had a impressive combat reckerd during the War. In total, 992 pilots graduated and flew aircraft in more then 1,578 war missions. In addition the men destroy 261 Enemy Aircraft, and was awerded 850 medals The group are one of the most deckerated units of the U.S. Army. Some pilots flyed as many as 100 missions—more than they were supposed to fly—because reinforsemints for the all black unit was scarce. The pilots remain active until 1946, well after the war had ended. Aside from the fact that they served honoribly they also paved the way for racial integration in the U.S. military.

WATCH FOR

- commas
- hyphens

MONDAY   Week 17

The Grossest Things

My family and ~~me~~ [I] went to Ireland on vacation last summer. That's where I experienced one of the most ~~sickning~~ [sickening] moments ever. Most of ireland was just ~~wanderfull~~ [wonderful] but then my Mom reminded me, that we were going to visit the Blarney Stone. I knew it was one of the most famous tourist spots in the country . . . and one of the ~~disgustingest~~ [most disgusting] spots, too. People ~~travels~~ [travel] from every where to kiss the Stone. By Kissing it you are supposed to magically get the "gift of the gab"—the ability to express yourself ~~good~~ [well]. People have been slobbering on that stone for ~~hunderds~~ [hundreds] of years. Yuck!

Error Summary

Capitalization	4
Language Usage	4
Punctuation:	
Comma	3
Exclamation Point	1
Quotation Mark	1
Spelling	4

TUESDAY   Week 17

Putting my lips on something that millions of other people had ~~kist~~ [kissed] didn't sound fun to me. Traveling to the castle where the blarney stone is, thoughts of running away ~~crossed my mind~~ [I had]. I wondered "how many people had kissed that stone? I kept picturing ~~a~~ [an] ugly, slimy rock with hundreds of year's worth of saliva on it. I also wondered "if anybody ever cleaned that stone." We arrived at the park, ~~payed~~ [paid] the fee, climbed to the top, and ~~we~~ stood in line. It was soon my turn to kiss the stone. So far, it is one of the grossest things I've done. As I mentioned, though, it is only one of the most disgusting places I've ~~visit~~ [visited].

Error Summary

Capitalization	2
Language Usage	2
Punctuation:	
Apostrophe	3
Comma	3
Period	1
Quotation Mark	3
Sentence Structure	2
Spelling	2

Name _____

The Grossest Things

My family and me went to Ireland on vacation last summer. That's where I experienced one of the most sickning moments ever. Most of ireland was just wanderfull but then my Mom reminded me, that we were going to visit the Blarney Stone. I knew it was one of the most famous tourist spots in the country . . . and one of the disgustingest spots, too. People travels from every where to kiss the Stone. By Kissing it you are supposed to magically get the "gift of the gab—the ability to express yourself good. People have been slobbering on that stone for hunderds of years. Yuck

- pronouns
- words that compare
- run-on sentences
- special phrases in quotation marks

Putting my lips on something that millions of other people had kist didnt sound fun to me. Traveling to the castle where the blarney stone is, thoughts of running away crossed my mind. I wondered "how many people had kissed that stone? I kept picturing a ugly slimy rock with hundreds of year's worth of saliva on it. I also wondered "if anybody ever cleaned that stone." We arrived at the park, payed the fee, climbed to the top, and we stood in line. It was soon my turn to kiss the stone. So far it is one of the grossest things I've done. As I mentioned, though it is only one of the most disgusting places Ive visit.

- apostrophes
- verbs
- dangling modifiers
- parallel structure

WEDNESDAY   Week 17

I recently went to Seattle washington to visit ~~relitives~~ relatives.
Strolling downtown, a curious thing ~~caught my attention~~. I saw I
wasn't even sure what I was seeing; the side of a brick
building was covered with thousands of blobs of ~~brilantly~~ brilliantly
colored tissue paper or ~~confety~~ confetti. ~~Fassinated~~ Fascinated, I ~~approach~~ approached the
wall to see what those blobs were. Were they buttons? Were
they flowers? What materials were they made from? Were
they made of cloth or plastic? I ~~skwinted~~ squinted, stepped closer and
examined the wall. It was at that ~~presise~~ precise moment that I
heard another ~~pedestrion~~ pedestrian yell from down the street, "look!
it's the world-famous Market Theater Gum Wall."

Error Summary

Capitalization	5
Language Usage	1
Punctuation:	
Apostrophe	1
Comma	3
Exclamation Point	2
Period	2
Question Mark	3
Sentence Structure	1
Spelling	7

THURSDAY   Week 17

since seeing (and nearly touching) the disgusting wall of
used gum in seattle I've been reading up on creepy ~~tourest~~ tourist
~~atractions~~ attractions. It turns out that there's an even ~~worst~~ worse wall of
gum in San Luis Obispo california. Called "Bubblegum Alley",
it's even bigger ~~then~~ than Seattles gum wall. The gobs of gum
~~reaches~~ reach 15 feet high and stretch for a ~~distinse~~ distance of 70 feet;
the history of the wall is ~~vayg~~ vague. Some people say it began in
the late 1940s; others say it ~~begun~~ began in the late 1950s. As for
me, it doesn't matter. I was just horrified that I almost
touched the gum wall. Then I remembered that I actually did
kiss the creepy blarney stone in ireland. Eww!

Error Summary

Capitalization	8
Language Usage	4
Punctuation:	
Apostrophe	4
Comma	3
Exclamation Point	1
Parentheses	1
Period	2
Quotation Mark	1
Spelling	4

WEDNESDAY   Week 17

I recently went to Seattle washington to visit relitives. Strolling downtown, a curious thing caught my attention. I wasnt even sure what I was seeing, the side of a brick building was covered with thousands of blobs of brilantly colored tissue paper or confety. Fassinated, I approach the wall. To see what those blobs were. Were they buttons. Were they flowers. What materials were they made from? Were they made of cloth or plastic. I skwinted, stepped closer and examined the wall. It was at that presise moment that I heard another pedestrion yell from down the street, "look. it's the world-famous Market Theater Gum Wall"

- dangling modifiers
- run-on sentences
- adverbs
- end punctuation
- articles

THURSDAY   Week 17

since seeing (and nearly touching the disgusting wall of used gum in seattle Ive been reading up on creepy tourest atractions. It turns out that theres an even worst wall of gum in San Luis Obispo california. Called "Bubblegum Alley", its even bigger then Seattles gum wall. The gobs of gum reaches 15 feet high, and stretch for a distinse of 70 feet, the history of the wall is vayg. Some people say it began in the late 1940s, others say it begun in the late 1950s. As for me, it doesn't matter. I was just horrified that I almost touched the gum wall. Then I remembered that I actually did kiss the creepy blarney stone in ireland. Eww

- place names
- apostrophes
- run-on sentences
- end punctuation

MONDAY   Week 18

The Transcontinental Railroad

The dream of building a ~~t~~Transcontinental ~~r~~Railroad ~~begun~~ began
in the 1830s, when steam ~~locamotives~~ locomotives were in use. In 1838,
planners met to discuss how to begin this important project.
The railroad would ~~joins~~ join the eastern and western United
states, and would be the biggest technological ~~endevver~~ endeavor of
the ~~c~~Century. Members of congress couldn't agree on the best
~~root~~ route for the railroad however. ~~Them~~ Those from the North ~~favered~~ favored
a northern route and those from the south, wanted ~~an~~ a
southern route. This wasn't surprising, given that towns along
the route would ~~devellop~~ develop and ~~prosspur~~ prosper from ~~commerse~~ commerce.

Error Summary

Capitalization	6
Language Usage	4
Punctuation:	
Apostrophe	2
Comma	4
Spelling	7

TUESDAY   Week 18

Congress had ~~antissipated~~ anticipated that the South would secede
from the union consequently representatives from the south
left Congress by 1861. Those from the north—the only ones
remaining—recognized that the railroad would have ~~a affect~~ an effect
on the outcome of the civil war which had just ~~began~~ begun. They
approved the bill for the pacific railway act, calling for the
construction of a railway line along a northern route. Then
president Abraham lincoln signed the bill on july 1, 1862. With
the passage of this bill, the Union Pacific Railroad Company
was incorporated and ~~were~~ was hired for the construction, along
with the central pacific railroad company.

Error Summary

Capitalization	15
Language Usage	4
Punctuation:	
Comma	3
Semicolon	1
Spelling	1

Name _____

The Transcontinental Railroad

The dream of building a Transcontinental Railroad begun in the 1830s, when steam locamotives were in use. In 1838, planners met to discuss how to begin this important project. The railroad would joins the eastern and western United states, and would be the biggest technological endevver of the Century. Members of congress couldnt agree on the best root for the railroad however. Them from the North favered a northern route and those from the south, wanted an southern route. This wasnt surprising, given that towns along the route would devellop and prosspur from commerse.

- place names
- geographic regions
- names of organizations
- pronouns

Congress had antissipated that the South would secede from the union consequently representatives from the south left Congress by 1861. Those from the north—the only ones remaining—recognized that the railroad would have a affect on the outcome of the civil war which had just began. They approved the bill for the pacific railway act, calling for the construction of a railway line along a northern route. Then president Abraham lincoln signed the bill on july 1 1862. With the passage of this bill, the Union Pacific Railroad Company was incorporated and were hired for the construction, along with the central pacific railroad company.

- semicolons
- historic events
- names of laws

WEDNESDAY   Week 18

The Central Pacific Railroad started in california and headed east the Union Pacific railroad began near omaha nebraska and hedded (headed) west. Construction in California began about six months after the President had signed legislation To allow the railroad to be builded (built). Why didnt it begin write (right) away. Manufactured goods had to be shipped to California first. Tons of rails, spikes and tools had to be sent by ship from the east coast. The panama canal hadnt yet been built in 1862 so the ships had to travel around south America to san francisco materials were sent from there by steamship up the sacramento river.

Error Summary

Capitalization	16
Language Usage	1
Punctuation:	
Apostrophe	2
Comma	4
Period	2
Question Mark	1
Semicolon	1
Spelling	2

THURSDAY   Week 18

Construction finally begun (began) in Sacramento California on january 8 1863, and near Omaha nebraska on december 2 1863. It would take about six years to finish the job. The tracks were finally joint (joined) on may 10 1869, at Promontory Point, Utah. As a sairamonial (ceremonial) gesture workers hammered in the last tie using a bronze spike and a gold spike. While construction were (was) taking place the railroad aided the North during the civil war. It also akselerated (accelerated) the pace at which the west was settled. Many years later interstate highways and air travel over shadowed the transcontinental railroad which faded into US history.

Error Summary

Capitalization	7
Language Usage	2
Punctuation:	
Comma	11
Period	2
Spelling	4

Daily Paragraph Editing • EMC 2838 • © Evan-Moor Corp.

Name _____

WEDNESDAY   Week 18

The Central Pacific Railroad started in california and headed east the Union Pacific railroad began near omaha nebraska and hedded west. Construction in California began about six months after the President had signed legislation. To allow the railroad to be builded. Why didnt it begin write away Manufactured goods had to be shipped to California first. Tons of rails, spikes and tools had to be sent by ship from the east coast. The panama canal hadnt yet been built in 1862 so the ships had to travel around south America to san francisco, materials were sent from there by steamship up the sacramento river.

- place names
- semicolons

THURSDAY   Week 18

Construction finally begun in Sacramento California on january 8 1863, and near Omaha nebraska on december 2 1863. It would take about six years to finish the job. The tracks were finally joint on may 10 1869, at Promontory Point, Utah. As a sairamonial gesture workers hammered in the last tie using a bronze spike and a gold spike. While construction were taking place the railroad aided the North during the civil war. It also akselerated the pace at which the west was settled. Many years later interstate highways and air travel over shadowed the transcontinental railroad which faded into US history.

- dates
- commas
- geographic regions
- abbreviations

MONDAY   Week 19

Stingray Migration

I will never ~~forgot~~ (forget) the day my family and ~~me~~ (I) found ~~ourselfs~~ (ourselves) right in the middle of a stingray migration. We were on a motorboat off the ¢oast of m̲exico. I was gazing at the sparkling, sapphire-blue water and turned away for a second. Glancing back to the water, an unusual sight ~~startled me~~ (I was startled by). It seemed as if a fluttering‸ flowing mass of golden ~~autumm~~ (autumn) leaves ~~were~~ (was) surrounding us⊙ thousands of diamond‿shaped figures moved ~~swift~~ (swiftly) in one direction. ~~Layars~~ (Layers) of gleaming stingrays fit ~~neat~~ (neatly) together over a blue background⊙ it was ~~an spektacyuler~~ (a spectacular) sight⊙

Error Summary

Capitalization	4
Language Usage	6
Punctuation:	
Comma	1
Hyphen	1
Period	3
Sentence Structure	1
Spelling	4

TUESDAY   Week 19

I was ~~ankshus~~ (anxious) to see how the stingrays moved through the water⊙ their flat bodies rode the ocean current, their backs toward the sun. The creatures flapped their wings like prehistoric birds, moving ~~flewidly~~ (fluidly) through an ~~atmusfear~~ (atmosphere) of salt water. ~~Occeassionally~~ (Occasionally), ~~a~~ (an) upturned wingtip pierced the water͐s surface like a shark͐s fin. The rays were moving at a determined pace, as if they all had one common goal. Each one trailed a wiry barbed "tail" behind it.

I was surprised by how close the ~~stringrays~~ (stingrays) had ~~came~~ (come) to the boat. They did not seem to fear us⁄0r even to notice ~~ourselves~~ (us) at all.

Error Summary

Capitalization	2
Language Usage	3
Punctuation:	
Apostrophe	2
Period	2
Quotation Mark	1
Spelling	5

MONDAY   **Week 19**

Stingray Migration

I will never forgot the day my family and me found ourselfs right in the middle of a stingray migration. We were on a motorboat off the Coast of mexico. I was gazing at the sparkling, sapphire-blue water and turned away for a second. Glancing back to the water, an unusual sight startled me. It seemed as if a fluttering flowing mass of golden autumm leaves were surrounding us, thousands of diamond shaped figures moved swift in one direction. Layars of gleaming stingrays fit neat together over a blue background it was an spektacyuler sight

WATCH FOR

- pronouns
- hyphens
- dangling modifiers
- run-on sentences

TUESDAY   **Week 19**

I was ankshus to see how the stingrays moved through the water, their flat bodies rode the ocean current, their backs toward the sun. The creatures flapped their wings like prehistoric birds, moving flewidly through an atmusfear of salt water. Occassionally, a upturned wingtip pierced the waters surface like a sharks fin. The rays were moving at a determined pace, as if they all had one common goal. Each one trailed a wiry barbed "tail behind it.

I was surprised by how close the stringrays had came to the boat. They did not seem to fear us. Or even to notice ourselves at all.

WATCH FOR

- run-on sentences
- special words in quotation marks
- pronouns

WEDNESDAY   Week 19

Curious to see the ever-moving stingrays up close, I
~~leened~~ *leaned* over the side of the boat with my camera to examine
them. Those stingrays had some very ~~distinktiv~~ *distinctive* features! ~~Its~~ *Their*
heads were dome-shaped. They had broad, blunt noses that
~~seperated~~ *separated* their inconspicuous eyes. When they ~~jump~~ *jumped* out of
the water, I could see their funny mouths; it looked as if
they were smiling. The rays were much ~~biggest~~ *bigger* than I
thought at first; their "wingspan" was about three feet.
Because the stingrays over lapped each other and turned
side ways as they ~~swum~~ *swam*, I could see that their undersides
~~was~~ *were* pale yellow, like buttercups.

Error Summary

Language Usage	5
Punctuation:	
Comma	4
Hyphen	1
Semicolon	1
Spelling	5

THURSDAY   Week 19

I wanted to remember the experience of ~~whitnesing~~ *witnessing*
a stingray migration. I stepped back from the edge of the
~~boat~~ *boat;* and ~~breethed~~ *breathed* the salt-scented air; it smelled like a
fishing trip. I welcomed the ~~sea~~ *Sea* ~~breeze~~ *Breeze;* the sun showered
us with a ~~fully~~ *full* serving of warmth.

In a flash, the ~~hord~~ *horde* of stingrays ~~were~~ *was* gone. The ocean
was solid blue once again; not a single hint of gold ~~remains~~ *remained*
in the water. The stingrays vanished as ~~rapid~~ *rapidly* as they had
appeared, and ~~their wasn't~~ *there was,* no sign that they had been there.
I will always remember the image of those diamond-shaped
figures racing ~~threw~~ *through* the water on that warm day.

Error Summary

Capitalization	3
Language Usage	5
Punctuation:	
Comma	2
Hyphen	2
Semicolon	3
Spelling	5

WEDNESDAY   Week 19

- hyphens
- verbs
- pronouns
- semicolons

Curious to see the ever moving stingrays up close I leened over the side of the boat with my camera to examine them. Those stingrays had some very distinktiv features! Its heads were dome-shaped. They had broad blunt noses that seperated their inconspicuous eyes. When they jump out of the water I could see their funny mouths; it looked as if they were smiling. The rays were much biggest than I thought at first, their "wingspan" was about three feet. Because the stingrays over lapped each other and turned side ways as they swum I could see that their undersides was pale yellow, like buttercups.

THURSDAY   Week 19

- run-on sentences
- hyphens
- semicolons
- double negatives

I wanted to remember the experience of whitnesing a stingray migration. I stepped back from the edge of the Boat, and breethed the salt scented air it smelled like a fishing trip. I welcomed the Sea Breeze the sun showered us with a fully serving of warmth.

In a flash, the hord of stingrays were gone. The ocean was solid blue once again, not a single hint of gold remains in the water. The stingrays vanished as rapid as they had appeared and their wasn't no sign that they had been there. I will always remember the image of those diamond shaped figures racing threw the water on that warm day.

MONDAY   Week 20

Bamboo Drift Racing

Sure, you've heard of basket ball and tennis, but have you ever heard of bamboo drift racing? It's an national sport in China, that requires skill, ballence, and strength. What exactly is bamboo drift racing? A person stands on a single pole (traditionally, bamboo) that floats in water (typically, on a river), and him or her paddles using a thin bamboo stick. The stick also helps for balance. Picture a tight-rope walker using a long stick for balance, and you'll get the idea. Compettiters race toward a finish line. Bamboo drifting is a time-honored activity. That evolved into a sport.

Error Summary

Capitalization	1
Language Usage	3
Punctuation:	
Apostrophe	3
Comma	3
Hyphen	2
Parentheses	1
Period	1
Question Mark	2
Spelling	3

TUESDAY   Week 20

Although some traditional aspecks of bamboo drifting have endured in the sport, others have changed. For example the essenshal motions and objektive remains the same; in both activities, the goal is to reach the destination while staying on the pole. One thing that has changed is the pole. Traditionally, bamboo drifters balansed on real bamboo poles. In the modern sport, a athlete stand on a narrow strip that resemble bamboo, but is actually made from fiberglass. This material is more durrible and buoyanter than bamboo. These properties of the material allows athletes to glide more smooth across the water.

Error Summary

Capitalization	2
Language Usage	7
Punctuation:	
Comma	4
Spelling	5

MONDAY   Week 20

WATCH FOR

- hyphens
- parentheses
- pronouns
- incomplete sentences

Bamboo Drift Racing

Sure, youve heard of basket ball and tennis, but have you ever heard of bamboo drift racing. Its an national sport in China, that requires skill ballence and strength. What exactly is bamboo drift racing. A person stands on a single pole (traditionally, bamboo) that floats in water (typically, on a river, and him or her paddles using a thin bamboo stick. The stick also helps for balance. Picture a tight rope walker using a long stick for balance, and youll get the idea. Compettiters race toward a finish line. Bamboo drifting is a time honored activity. That evolved into a sport.

TUESDAY   Week 20

WATCH FOR

- incomplete sentences
- verbs
- words that compare

Although some traditional aspecks of bamboo drifting have endured in the sport. Others have changed. For example the essenshal motions and objektive remains the same; in both activities, the goal is to reach the destination while staying on the pole. One thing that has changed, is the pole. Traditionally, bamboo drifters balansed on real bamboo poles. In the modern sport, a athlete stand on a narrow strip that resemble bamboo, but is actually made from Fiberglass. This material is more durrible and buoyanter than bamboo. These properties of the material allows athletes to glide more smooth across the water.

WEDNESDAY　　　　　　　　　　　　　　　　Week 20

You may be wondering why bamboo was used in the first place? In the southern provinsse [province] of Guizhou (gwee-jo), where bamboo drift racing began bamboo is plentifull [plentiful] and easy [easily] accessible—especially a variety called moso. This is the larger [largest] of all bamboo species' that grows [grow] in temperite [temperate] regions such as guizhou. Canes of moso bamboo can grew [grow] to be very large (as much as 92 feet [28 meters] tall and more then [than] 7 inches [18 centamiters [centimeters]] thick. A cane of moso bamboo can support as much as 165 pounds (about 75 kilograms) of weight. Its strength and accessibility therefore make moso bamboo a perfect material for drifting.

Error Summary

Capitalization	1
Language Usage	5
Punctuation:	
Apostrophe	1
Bracket	1
Comma	3
Parentheses	2
Period	2
Spelling	4

THURSDAY　　　　　　　　　　　　　　　　Week 20

Bamboo drifting has ganed [gained] more attention since the 2011 National traditional ethnic Sports Games in china This event feechured [featured] the first national compitition [competition] for the sport. Athleets [Athletes] competed in a 60-meter race or a 100-meter race there were mens and womens Divisions for these catigories [categories]. All of the racers used fiberglass poles of a consisstant [consistent] length (7.5 meters. One competitor said that preparing for the sport was exhausting he trained about seven hours every day for several Months. "The hardest part," he explained, "Is balancing." He often practiced on land using a large ball. "The principal [principle] of maintaining balance, he said is the same."

Error Summary

Capitalization	6
Punctuation:	
Apostrophe	2
Comma	1
Hyphen	2
Parentheses	1
Period	1
Quotation Mark	3
Semicolon	2
Spelling	7

WEDNESDAY   Week 20

- parentheses
- brackets
- apostrophes
- words that compare

You may be wondering why bamboo was used in the first place? In the southern provinsse of Guizhou (gwee-jo), where bamboo drift racing began bamboo is plentifull and easy accessible—especially a variety called moso. This is the larger of all bamboo species' that grows in temperite regions such as guizhou. Canes of moso bamboo can grew to be very large (as much as 92 feet [28 meters] tall and more then 7 inches [18 centamiters thick. A cane of moso bamboo can support as much as 165 pounds about 75 kilograms) of weight. Its strength and accessibility therefore make moso bamboo a perfect material for drifting

THURSDAY   Week 20

- events
- hyphens
- semicolons
- quotation marks

Bamboo drifting has ganed more attention since the 2011 National traditional ethnic Sports Games in china This event feechured the first national compitition for the sport. Athleets competed in a 60 meter race or a 100 meter race there were mens and womens Divisions for these catigories. All of the racers used fiberglass poles of a consisstant length (7.5 meters. One competitor said that preparing for the sport was exhausting he trained about seven hours every day for several Months. "The hardest part," he explained, "Is balancing." He often practiced on land using a large ball. The principal of maintaining balance, he said is the same."

MONDAY   Week 21

Letters from Panama

january 10 1906

dear Amelia,

the ~~voyidge~~ *voyage* was long but I finally arrived in panamas canal zone many other workers have ~~came~~ *come* here for jobs *like me* like me. Although the work will be ~~strennuous~~ *strenuous* and laden with peril the wages are good. When the canal is ~~finnished~~ *finished* ships will no longer have to sail around south america. I miss my family, but I'm fine things arent bad for us here in Panama

Your loving Husband,

samuel

Error Summary

Capitalization	10
Language Usage	1
Punctuation:	
Apostrophe	2
Comma	4
Period	3
Sentence Structure	1
Spelling	3

TUESDAY   Week 21

march 17 1906

Dear Amelia

The ~~acomodations~~ *accommodations* here are comfortable enough the company provides three cooked meals a day at a reasonable price. Working conditions are fair; ~~saftey~~ *safety* is rightfully a ~~consurn~~ *concern* to all. Most laborers work six days a week the men gather on sundays to play chess or maybe even baseball. A few men in the barracks have ~~became~~ *become* ill with yellow fever Dont worry about me. Im taking ~~meassures~~ *measures* to stay healthy.

Much love

Samuel

Error Summary

Capitalization	4
Language Usage	1
Punctuation:	
Apostrophe	2
Comma	4
Period	3
Spelling	4

MONDAY   Week 21

- dates
- run-on sentences
- misplaced modifiers
- commas

Letters from Panama

january 10 1906

dear Amelia,

the voyidge was long but I finally arrived in panamas canal zone many other workers have came here for jobs like me. Although the work will be strennuous and laden with peril the wages are good. When the canal is finnished ships will no longer have to sail around south america. I miss my family, but I'm fine, things arent bad for us here in Panama

Your loving Husband,

samuel

TUESDAY   Week 21

- commas
- apostrophes
- run-on sentences

march 17 1906,

Dear Amelia

The acomodations here are comfortable enough, the company provides three cooked meals a day at a reasonable price. Working conditions are fair; saftey is rightfully a consurn to all. Most laborers work six days a week, the men gather on sundays to play chess or maybe even baseball. A few men in the barracks have became ill with yellow fever Dont worry about me. Im taking meassures to stay healthy.

Much love:

Samuel

WEDNESDAY — Week 21

april 15, 1906

Dear amelia:

Despite outbreak's of disease in the barracks, I am in ~~exellent~~ excellent health. My good friend martin is suffering with Yellow Fever. In the beginning, he had ~~a~~ an awful headache and great thirst. Yesterday he was delirious, ~~speaks~~ spoke aimlessly and had yellowish skin. We gave him a mustard bath, but it didnt help much. People say that mosquitoes spread yellow fever. Good grief! This hot ~~hummid~~ humid place is filled with mosquitoes!

Love,
sam

Error Summary

Capitalization	6
Language Usage	2
Punctuation:	
Apostrophe	2
Comma	8
Exclamation Point	1
Spelling	2

THURSDAY — Week 21

may 20, 1906

Dear Amelia,

Thankfully, martin has recovered. Hooray! Many american workers, though, are leaving panama because of yellow fever, malaria, and other ~~contajuss~~ contagious diseases, which ~~spreads~~ spread especially fast in the cramped barracks, where living conditions are ~~worst~~ worse than elsewhere. The "mosquito ~~briggades~~ brigades," which were organized last year, ~~periodicly~~ periodically fumigate areas to reduce mosquito populations. Things should gradually improve for us.

Yours Truly,
Samuel

Error Summary

Capitalization	7
Language Usage	2
Punctuation:	
Comma	5
Exclamation Point	1
Period	2
Quotation Mark	1
Spelling	3

WEDNESDAY   Week 21

april 15 1906

Dear amelia;

    Despite outbreak's of disease in the barracks. I am in exellent health. My good friend martin is suffering with Yellow Fever. In the beginning, he had a awful headache and great thirst. Yesterday he was delirious speaks aimlessly and had yellowish skin. We gave him a mustard bath but it didnt help much. People say that mosquitoes spread yellow fever. Good grief. This hot hummid place is filled with mosquitoes!

      Love

      sam

- personal names
- incomplete sentences
- commas
- end punctuation

THURSDAY   Week 21

may 20 1906

Dear Amelia—

    Thankfully, martin has recovered. Hooray. Many american workers, though, are leaving panama. Because of yellow fever malaria and other contajuss diseases, which spreads especially fast in the cramped barracks. Where living conditions are worst than elsewhere. The "mosquito briggades", which were organized last year, periodicly fumigate areas to reduce mosquito populations. Things should gradually improve for us.

      Yours Truly

      Samuel

- end punctuation
- commas
- incomplete sentences

MONDAY   Week 22

A "Fuller" Challenge

Long before the ~~developpment~~ development of the "green building"

movement, Buckminster Fuller was designing energy-efficient

buildings. A twentieth-century inventor, Fuller ~~seeked~~ sought to

~~adress~~ address important economic, scientific, and cultural issues, with

his inventions. He saw that the world's resources (such as

fuel, water, lumber, and metals) were limited. He also noticed

that society's use of ~~tecknology~~ technology often ~~were~~ was not in ~~harmuny~~ harmony

with nature. ~~Solveing~~ Solving this problem, he thought, would protect

the planet and improve society. Mostly, Fuller wanted to

foster a world in which people cared for the environment.

Error Summary

Language Usage	2
Punctuation:	
Apostrophe	2
Comma	9
Hyphen	2
Period	2
Spelling	5

TUESDAY   Week 22

In ~~tradishunal~~ traditional home construction, builder's bring lumber,

and other materials to the site, cut pieces as needed, and

~~they~~ throw away what they don't use. Tons of scraps—even

usable ones—end up in landfills. Also, many materials contain

toxins such as formaldehyde and chlorinated plastics. The

more materials builders waste, the ~~worst~~ worse it is for the

environment. Fuller believed that if the Construction Industry

changed its ~~methids~~ methods, ~~less~~ fewer materials would be wasted and

safer structures would be built. So he designed affordable,

~~effishunt~~ efficient houses that would be produced in a ~~facterry~~ factory and

shipped to the building ~~sight~~ site.

Error Summary

Capitalization	2
Language Usage	2
Punctuation:	
Apostrophe	2
Comma	2
Dash	1
Sentence Structure	1
Spelling	5

Name _____

A "Fuller" Challenge

Long before the developpment of the "green building" movement Buckminster Fuller was designing energy efficient buildings. A twentieth century inventor, Fuller seeked to adress important economic scientific and cultural issues, with his inventions. He saw that the worlds resources (such as fuel water lumber and metals) were limited He also noticed that societys use of tecknology often were not in harmuny with nature. Solveing this problem he thought would protect the planet and improve society Mostly, Fuller wanted to foster a world in which people cared for the environment.

- commas
- hyphens

In tradishunal home construction, builder's bring lumber, and other materials to the site, cut pieces as needed, and they throw away what they dont use. Tons of scraps—even usable ones end up in landfills. Also, many materials contain toxins such as formaldehyde and chlorinated plastics. The more materials builders waste, the worst it is for the environment. Fuller believed that if the Construction Industry changed its methids, less materials would be wasted and safer structures would be built. So he designed affordable effishunt houses that would be produced in a facterry and shipped to the building sight.

- parallel structure
- dashes
- commas
- adjectives

WEDNESDAY   Week 22

People often link buckminster fuller with a structure called a "geodesic dome. Actually the first so-called geodesic dome was designed by dr walther bauersfeld a german engineer. His design inspired Fuller who applied for u.s. patents and popularized the structure. The geodesic dome is a rounded, three-dimensional shape consisting of identicle [identical] equilateral triangles. (when completed, it forms a sphere.) The rijud [rigid] triangle gives the dome its strength. The dome unlike a rectangyuler [rectangular] building can support its own wait [weight], No matter how big it is. One well-known geodesic dome is Spaceship Earth at epcot in florida.

Error Summary

Capitalization	12
Punctuation:	
Comma	5
Hyphen	3
Period	1
Quotation Mark	1
Spelling	4

THURSDAY   Week 22

Buckminster Fuller died in 1983. One of his legacys [legacies] however is the annuel [annual] Buckminster Fuller Challenge. Its a contest that offers new inventors and dreamers the chance to develop and implumment [implement] their ideas for solving some of the worlds most challenging problems. The contest was established by the buckminster fuller institute in brooklyn New York. Every year, contestants submit designs that addresses [address] a specific critical issue effecting [affecting] humanity. The winner (a person or a team of people) receive [receives] a cash prize that will help fund the winning idea. Thanks to Fullers work the future holds creative posabilities [possibilities] and solutions.

Error Summary

Capitalization	4
Language Usage	3
Punctuation:	
Apostrophe	3
Comma	4
Parentheses	1
Spelling	4

WEDNESDAY   Week 22

People often link buckminster fuller with a structure called a "geodesic dome. Actually the first so called geodesic dome was designed by dr walther bauersfeld a german engineer. His design inspired Fuller who applied for u.s. patents and popularized the structure. The geodesic dome is a rounded, three dimensional shape consisting of identicle equilateral triangles. (when completed, it forms a sphere.) The rijud triangle gives the dome its strength. The dome unlike a rectangyuler building can support its own wait, No matter how big it is. One well known geodesic dome is Spaceship Earth at epcot in florida.

- punctuation with quotation marks
- hyphens
- personal names
- place names

THURSDAY   Week 22

Buckminster Fuller died in 1983. One of his legacys however is the annuel Buckminster Fuller Challenge. Its a contest that offers new inventors and dreamers the chance to develop and implumment their ideas for solving some of the worlds most challenging problems. The contest was established by the buckminster fuller institute in brooklyn New York. Every year, contestants submit designs that addresses a specific critical issue effecting humanity. The winner (a person or a team of people receive a cash prize that will help fund the winning idea. Thanks to Fullers work the future holds creative posabilities and solutions.

- hyphens
- verbs
- names of organizations
- place names

MONDAY   Week 23

Error Summary

Capitalization	5
Punctuation:	
Apostrophe	1
Comma	1
Hyphen	2
Period	1
Spelling	7

Ten-Day Traffic Jam Ends

August 25, 2010. A 60-mile traffic jam that began on august 13 on China National Highway 110 between the cities of beijing and zhangjiakou (jung-jyah-ko) finally appears to be breaking up after ten days. The bumper-to-bumper traffic jam has involved more than 10,000 vehicles. On a major route leading into China's capital. On average cars and trucks have traveled only a third of a mile a day. On the tenth day, local authorities commissioned 400 police officers to patrol the crowded highway. Stranded motorists are growing increasingly discouraged and concerned.

TUESDAY   Week 23

Error Summary

Capitalization	2
Language Usage	4
Punctuation:	
Apostrophe	1
Comma	3
Period	2
Spelling	6

Long lines of cars, trucks, and vans fill the lanes of the highway. Police officers report that traffic is often at a complete standstill for several hours at a time. Motorists are sleeping in their cars. And taking crude showers on the side of the road. Some drivers are passing the time by playing card games, relaxing on the ground next to their automobiles. They remain alert to the possibility that the traffic will start moving again. Along the highway, vendors from nearby villages have set up stalls, and are selling food and beverages at inflated prices. These vendors on the outskirts of town know that hungry drivers have few other options.

Name _____

Ten-Day Traffic Jam Ends

August 25, 2010. A 60 mile traffic jam that began on august 13 on China National Highway 110 between the cities of beijing and zhangjiakou (jung-jyah-ko) finally appears to be breaking up after ten days. The bumper-to bumper traffic jam has involved more than 10,000 vehicals. On a major route leading into Chinas cappital. On average cars and trucks have traveled only a third of a mile a day. On the tenth day, local authoratees comisioned 400 Police offisers to patrol the crowded highway. Stranded motorists are growing increasingly discouridged and conserned.

WATCH FOR

- hyphens
- place names
- incomplete sentences

Long lines of cars trucks and vans fills the lanes of the highway. Police officers report that traffic are often at a compleat standstill For several hours at a time. Motarists are sleeping in their cars. And taking crood showers on the side of the road. Some drivers are passing the time by playing card games, relaxing on the ground next to their automobiles. They remain allert to the possibility that the traffic will starts moving again. Along the highway, vendors from nearby villages have set up stalls, and are selling food and bevridges at inflated prices. These vendors on the outscurts of town knows that hungry driver's have few other options

WATCH FOR

- commas
- verbs
- incomplete sentences

WEDNESDAY   Week 23

Scheduled lane closures due to roadwork, which ~~begun~~ *began*

on ~~august~~ 13, ~~was~~ *were* the primary cause of the traffic jam.

According to highway officials, traffic ~~practikly~~ *practically* came to a halt

within hours after the road construction began. The roadwork,

which is ongoing through ~~september~~ will repair pothole's and

crack's caused by large trucks carrying heavy loads. Ironically,

the same trucks that caused the damage ~~has~~ *have* been sitting in

this ~~masive~~ *massive* traffic jam. Roadwork is only one ~~facter~~ *factor*, though.

This highway ~~regulerly~~ *regularly* sees a high ~~volyoom~~ *volume* of traffic daily. It

happens to be a common tourist route leading to a ~~populer~~ *popular*

section of China's great wall.

Error Summary
Capitalization	4
Language Usage	3
Punctuation:	
Apostrophe	3
Comma	3
Spelling	6

THURSDAY   Week 23

When asked why they don't simply find a ~~alternut~~ *an alternate* route,

some drivers claim that it would mean traveling farther, which

would be ~~expensiver~~ *more expensive*. Others ~~explains~~ *explain* that big trucks ~~eksede~~ *exceed*

the weight limits on Beijing's side roads.

Road construction is ~~skeduled~~ *scheduled* to be completed by the

end of ~~september~~. Traffic on this highway will be ~~releeved~~ *relieved*

at that time. However, with car sales on the rise in China,

lengthy traffic jams are likely to be ~~commoner~~ *more common* in the future.

Niu Fengrui, ~~a~~ *an* expert on urban planning in ~~beijing~~, is cynical.

"If there were no traffic jams in the city," he jokes, "that

would be news."

Error Summary
Capitalization	2
Language Usage	5
Punctuation:	
Apostrophe	2
Comma	4
Quotation Mark	2
Spelling	4

WEDNESDAY   Week 23

Scheduled lane closures due to roadwork, which begun on august 13, was the primary cause of the traffic jam. According to highway officials traffic practikly came to a halt within hours after the road construction began. The roadwork which is ongoing through september will repair pothole's and crack's caused by large trucks carrying heavy loads. Ironically, the same trucks that caused the damage has been sitting in this masive traffic jam. Roadwork is only one facter, though. This highway regulerly sees a high volyoom of traffic daily. It happens to be a common tourist route leading to a populer section of Chinas great wall.

- verbs
- dates
- commas

THURSDAY   Week 23

When asked why they dont simply find a alternut route some drivers claim that it would mean traveling farther which would be expensiver. Others explains that big trucks eksede the weight limits on Beijings side roads.

Road construction is skeduled to be completed by the end of september. Traffic on this highway will be releeved at that time. However, with car sales on the rise in China lengthy traffic jams are likely to be commoner in the future. Niu Fengrui, a expert on urban planning in beijing is cynical. "If there were no traffic jams in the city, he jokes, "that would be news.

- articles
- commas
- words that compare
- quotation marks

MONDAY	Week 24

A Not-So-Sweet Story

Diabetes ~~are~~ *is* on the rise in the united states—not just for ^Adults but also for ^Teens. Diabetes is a serious condition, in which the level of glucose, or sugar, in the blood is too high. The body ~~normaly regulate~~ *normally regulates* its own blood glucose level; the pancreas (an organ near the kidneys) ~~produce~~ *produces* insulin (~~an~~ *a* ^Hormone that helps convert glucose into energy). With diabetes, this process ~~don't~~ *doesn't* work properly; glucose stay's unused in the blood. It ~~coat~~ *coats* red blood cells, causing them to stick to the blood ~~vesel~~ *vessel* walls and to block ~~surkyulation~~ *circulation*. Thin, blood vessels in the eyes, feet, and kidney's are most at risk.

Error Summary

Capitalization	5
Language Usage	6
Punctuation:	
Apostrophe	2
Comma	4
Parentheses	1
Period	1
Spelling	3

TUESDAY	Week 24

There are three main types of diabetes—type 1, type 2, and gestational diabetes. In type 1, the pancreas ~~produce~~ *produces* almost no insulin at all. In type 2, the body produces insulin, but can't process it ~~good~~ *well*. Gestational diabetes ~~occur~~ *occurs* during a woman's pregnancy. A woman with gestational diabetes has a ~~more great~~ *greater* risk for the rest of her life of developing type 2 diabetes; she also ~~pass~~ *passes* this risk on to the child. People who have type 1 diabetes must add insulin to the body—usually through injection. People who have type 2 diabetes ~~usual~~ *usually* take pills to regulate the body's use of insulin.

Error Summary

Capitalization	1
Language Usage	6
Punctuation:	
Apostrophe	3
Comma	3
Dash	1
Period	2

Name _____

- verbs
- parentheses
- commas

A Not-So-Sweet Story

Diabetes are on the rise in the united states—not just for Adults but also for Teens. Diabetes is a serious condition. in which the level of glucose, or sugar in the blood is too high. The body normaly regulate its own blood glucose level; the pancreas (an organ near the kidneys) produce insulin (an Hormone that helps convert glucose into energy. With diabetes, this process don't work properly; glucose stay's unused in the blood. It coat red blood cells, causing them to stick to the blood vesel walls and to block surkyulation. Thin, blood vessels in the eyes feet and kidney's are most at risk.

- dashes
- commas
- adverbs
- words that compare

There are three main types of diabetes type 1 type 2 and gestational diabetes. In type 1, the pancreas produce almost no insulin at all. In type 2, the body produces insulin, but cant process it good. Gestational diabetes occur during a womans pregnancy. A woman with gestational diabetes has a more great risk for the rest of her life of developing type 2 diabetes, she also pass this risk on to the child. People who have type 1 diabetes must add insulin to the body—usually through injection. People who have type 2 diabetes usual take pills to regulate the bodys use of insulin?

WEDNESDAY　　　　　　　　　　　Week 24

The causes of diabetes is [are] not fully understood. We do know that type 1 can be cause [caused] by something in a person's genetic makeup; Viruses and Toxins may also be factors. As for type 2 diabetes, we know that this chronic disease is linked to obesity, inactivity and genetics. Some people believe that indulgeing [indulging] in too much sugar cause [causes] diabetes. This is not strickly [strictly] true, however eating a eksessive [an excessive] amount of sugar is not good for anyone, because it can increase blood glucose levels and can contribbute [contribute] to weight gain. many [Many] nutritionists' recommends [recommend] that people eat good carbohydrates, such as whole grains, lowfat milk, and fresh fruits and veggetables [vegetables].

Error Summary

Capitalization	4
Language Usage	5
Punctuation:	
Apostrophe	2
Comma	3
Period	1
Spelling	5

THURSDAY　　　　　　　　　　　Week 24

Other than eating healthful foods and regular meals what can people do if they have diabetes? The goal should be to prevent spikes in blood glucose levels. Here is [are] just a few guide lines for maintaining steddy [steady] levels:

• Do something physical [physically] active each day.

• Maintain an [a] healthy weight.

• You should check your blood glucose level's [levels] reggularly [regularly].

• Take medications as perscribed [prescribed].

Actually, these simple guidelines apply to all indivijewels [individuals] (whether they are at risk for diabetes or not) In general, people can make many choises [choices] that lead to a healthy life!

Error Summary

Language Usage	3
Punctuation:	
Apostrophe	1
Comma	3
Parentheses	1
Period	2
Question Mark	1
Sentence Structure	1
Spelling	6

Name _____

- verbs
- apostrophes

The causes of diabetes is not fully understood. We do know that type 1 can be cause by something in a persons genetic makeup; Viruses and Toxins may also be factors. As for type 2 diabetes, we know that this chronic disease is linked to obesity, inactivity and genetics. Some people believe that indulgeing in too much sugar cause diabetes. This is not strickly true, however eating a eksessive amount of sugar is not good for anyone, because it can increase blood glucose levels and can contribbute to weight gain. many nutritionists' recommends that people eat good carbohydrates, such as whole grains lowfat milk, and fresh fruits and veggetables.

- end punctuation
- parallel structure
- parentheses

Other than eating healthful foods and regular meals what can people do if they have diabetes The goal should be to prevent spikes in blood glucose levels. Here is just a few guide lines for maintaining steddy levels:

- Do something physical active each day.
- Maintain an healthy weight.
- You should check your blood glucose level's reggularly.
- Take medications as perscribed

Actually these simple guidelines apply to all indivijewels. (whether they are at risk for diabetes or not. In general people can make many choises that lead to a healthy life!

MONDAY　　　　　　　　　　　　　　　Week 25

Taking "The Rock"

The international Occupy Movement that ~~begun~~ [began] in 2011 certainly was not the first movement in which individuals gathered together and ~~forming~~ [formed] unified groups to occupy ~~publick~~ [public] lands in protest. On ~~november~~ 20 1969 a group of ~~american~~ ~~indians~~ occupied ~~alcatraz~~ ~~island~~ in the San Francisco Bay. A member of the ~~mohawk~~ tribe, ~~richard~~ ~~oakes~~, got a ~~charder~~ [charter] boat, and ~~leaded~~ [led] an expedition to the ~~Island~~. Oakes ~~were~~ [was] accompanied by American ~~indian~~, college students from the Bay Area. The group was symbolically claiming the island (once belonging to the Ohlone). On ~~behaff~~ [behalf] of all tribes.

TUESDAY　　　　　　　　　　　　　　　Week 25

The group called itself "Indian's of All Tribes" and was soon joined by more supporters from across the country. In all, about 100 American Indians ~~occupyed~~ [occupied] the island in a ~~demonstrashun~~ [demonstration] that lasted until ~~june~~ 11 1971. One of ~~there~~ [their] purposes ~~were~~ [was] to draw attention to the ~~plite~~ [plight] of the ~~american~~ ~~indian~~. They demanded compensation for the many treaties ~~breaked~~ [broken] by the U.S. government. Referring ~~specific~~ [specifically] to the 1868 Treaty of ~~fort~~ ~~laramie~~ (a peace ~~agreament~~ [agreement] between the ~~US~~ government and the ~~sioux~~), they ~~ask~~ [asked] for all abandoned retired, or unused ~~fedural~~ [federal] lands to be ~~return~~ [returned] to the tribes they had been ~~stealed~~ [stolen] from.

MONDAY   **Week 25**

Taking "The Rock"

The international Occupy Movement that begun in 2011 certainly was not the first movement in which individuals gathered together and forming unified groups to occupy publick lands in protest. On november 20 1969 a group of american indians occupied alcatraz island in the San Francisco Bay. A member of the mohawk tribe, richard oakes, got a charder boat, and leaded an expedition to the Island. Oakes were accompanied by American indian, college students from the Bay Area The group was symbolically claiming the island (once belonging to the Ohlone). On behaff of all tribes.

- verbs
- dates
- place names
- ethnic groups

TUESDAY   **Week 25**

The group called itself Indian's of All Tribes" and was soon joined by more supporters from across the country. In all, about 100 American Indians occupied the island in a demonstrashun that lasted until june 11 1971. One of there purposes were to draw attention to the plite of the american indian. They demanded compensation for the many treaties breaked by the U.S. government. Referring specific to the 1868 Treaty of fort laramie (a peace agreament between the US government and the sioux), they ask for all abandoned retired, or unused fedural lands to be return to the tribes they had been stealed from.

- special phrases in quotation marks
- dates
- names of laws
- adverbs

WEDNESDAY   Week 25

The Indians of All tribes claimed that alcatraz met
some of the criterea [criteria] cited in the treaty of fort laramie.
However, the Treaty clear [clearly] applied only to the Sioux Nation,
and to a particular geographical area occupied by the sioux.
Still, the demonstraighters [demonstrators] claimed Alcatraz as their own,
citing the "right of discovery". In his book The Occupation of
Alcatraz Island, historian troy r Johnson discusses this idea.
He writes, "Indigenous peoples had been traveling to Alcatraz
Island for 10,000 . . years before europeans ever entered the
San Francisco Bay Area." Johnsons interpretation suggest [suggests] that
American Indians were justafyed [justified] in occupying Alcatraz.

Error Summary

Capitalization	10
Language Usage	2
Punctuation:	
Apostrophe	1
Comma	2
Ellipses	1
Period	1
Quotation Mark	2
Underlined Words	5
Spelling	3

THURSDAY   Week 25

The occupiers requested many things but its [their] demands
were'nt [weren't] met. They wanted the deed to Alcatraz island; they
also ask [asked] to establich a [establish an] American Indian university, a cultural
center, and a museum. The government refuzed [refused], insisting
that the occupiers leave. Eventully [Eventually], the government cut off
electrical power, And took away the supply of fresh water.
Still, the movement helped the occupiers accomplish one of
their major goals: to obtain tribal sovereignty on tribal land's.
(In other words, they got the U.S. government to allow tribes
to govern theirselves [themselves].) The movement also led to a greater
awearness, [awareness] of American Indian identaty [identity] and culture.

Error Summary

Capitalization	4
Language Usage	4
Punctuation:	
Apostrophe	1
Comma	3
Parentheses	1
Period	3
Spelling	6

Name _____

The Indians of All tribes claimed that alcatraz met some of the criterea cited in the treaty of fort laramie. However the Treaty clear applied only to the Sioux Nation, and to a particular geographical area occupied by the sioux. Still, the demonstraighters claimed Alcatraz as their own, citing the "right of discovery". In his book The Occupation of Alcatraz Island, historian troy r Johnson discusses this idea. He writes, Indigenous peoples had been traveling to Alcatraz Island for 10,000 . . years before europeans ever entered the San Francisco Bay Area." Johnsons interpretation suggest that American Indians were justafyed in occupying Alcatraz.

- names of organizations
- book titles
- abbreviations
- ellipses

The occupiers requested many things but its demands were'nt met. They wanted the deed to Alcatraz island; they also ask to establich a American Indian university a cultural Center, and a museum The government refuzed, insisting that the occupiers leave. Eventully, the Government cut off electrical power. And took away the supply of fresh water. Still, the movement helped the occupiers accomplish one of their major goals: to obtain tribal sovereignty on tribal land's (In other words, they got the U.S. government to allow tribes to govern theirselves. The movement also led to a greater awearness, of American Indian identaty and culture.

- possessives
- incomplete sentences
- parentheses

MONDAY   Week 26

Gardeners' Blog

Posted by JulieGreenThumb on june 10 2012, at 12 43 P.M.

Well Im excited that my vegetable garden is doing so well.
are
There is kale, squash, corn cucumbres *(cucumbers)*, and more. My tomatoe *(tomato)*

plants are producing a lot of fruit Ill have to give tomatoes
recently
away! I recent went to boston and toured the Fenway Victory

Gardens residents can get their own garden plots there.
People
Peoples sure do some creative things! In one plot I saw wind
silverware
chimes made of silverweare. Another plot had a *(an)* old lawn
flowers
chair with beautiful flours growing through it the gardens
grow   *edible*
inspired me to growing more eddable plants next year.

Error Summary

Capitalization	4
Language Usage	5
Punctuation:	
Apostrophe	2
Colon	1
Comma	3
Period	3
Spelling	5

TUESDAY   Week 26

Posted by GreenFred on June, 11, 2012 at 1 15 A.m.

Congratulations on your tomatoes Julie! I completely agree with
inspirational
you about the Fenway victory gardens being insperrational. I
fortunate
was fortchunate to visit the gardens last year and saw many
varieties
different verieties of plants beets, Swiss chard, squash basil

and potatoes, to name a few. The gardens provide fruits and

vegetables to many of bostons home less shelters, and soup

kitchens. They inspired me to start growing mush rooms
even
lettuce, and beans. I planted a pear tree even! Its rewarding

to grow your own food I really enjoy it but I wish I were
more creative
creativer at decorating my garden

Error Summary

Capitalization	4
Language Usage	1
Punctuation:	
Apostrophe	2
Colon	1
Comma	8
Dash	1
Period	2
Sentence Structure	1
Spelling	5

Name _____

Gardeners' Blog

Posted by JulieGreenThumb on june 10 2012, at 12 43 P.M.

Well Im excited that my vegetable garden is doing so well. There is kale, squash, corn cucumbres, and more. My tomatoe plants are producing a lot of fruit, Ill have to give tomatoes away! I recent went to boston and toured the Fenway Victory Gardens, residents can get their own garden plots there. Peoples sure do some creative things! In one plot I saw wind chimes made of silverweare. Another plot had a old lawn chair with beautiful flours growing through it, the gardens inspired me to growing more eddable plants next year.

WATCH FOR

- dates
- time
- adverbs
- run-on sentences

Posted by GreenFred on June, 11, 2012 at 1 15 A.m.

Congratulations on your tomatoes Julie! I completely agree with you about the Fenway victory gardens being insperrational. I was fortchunate to visit the gardens last year and saw many different verieties of plants beets, Swiss chard, squash basil and potatoes, to name a few. The gardens provide fruits and vegetables to many of bostons home less shelters, and soup kitchens. They inspired me to start growing mush rooms lettuce, and beans. I planted a pear tree even! Its rewarding to grow your own food I really enjoy it but I wish I were creativer at decorating my garden

WATCH FOR

- dashes
- dates
- time
- misplaced modifiers

WEDNESDAY   Week 26

Posted by Gardenia on june 11, 2012, at 7:10 A.M.

Hey, GreenFred! I'm a garden decorator! Using an old chair

to ~~enhances~~ enhance a garden is a good idea. I often place discarded

items in the garden. My kids and ~~me~~ I collect used coffee

cans and make planter's out of them. (You can also use old

rain boots or toy wagons for this ~~perpose~~ purpose.) We've also made

birdhouses from coffee cans and one-gallon milk containers.

Posted by VegFan on June 12, 2012, at 9:36 A.M.

Hello! I have a question for Gardenia. I've been having a

problem ~~rescently~~ recently with bird's and squirrels' getting into my

yard and eating the plants. What can I do to stop them?

Error Summary

Capitalization	1
Language Usage	2
Punctuation:	
Apostrophe	6
Comma	2
Hyphen	1
Parentheses	1
Period	3
Question Mark	1
Spelling	2

THURSDAY   Week 26

Posted by Gardenia on June 12, 2012, at 10:01 a.m.

Hi, VegFan. Try hanging shiny objects (such as old CDs or

aluminum pie plates) around ~~you're~~ your yard to scare the animals.

The sun light reflecting off ~~this~~ these items should sufficiently

~~startel~~ startle the ~~creetures~~ creatures and make ~~'em leaf~~ them leave your garden.

Posted by Planty on June, 14, 2012, at 5:24 p.M.

~~I~~ I've been bothered for years with critters' getting into my

garden. One thing that ~~work~~ works is soaking some rags in ~~vinigar~~ vinegar,

and placing the rags around the plant's that the critters like.

The smell ~~drive~~ drives them away. sprinkling coffee grounds on the

soil has the same effect.

Error Summary

Capitalization	4
Language Usage	5
Punctuation:	
Apostrophe	2
Colon	1
Comma	7
Parentheses	1
Period	1
Spelling	6

WEDNESDAY　　　　　　　　　　　　　　　Week 26

WATCH FOR

- commas
- pronouns
- parentheses
- hyphens

Posted by Gardenia on june 11 2012, at 7:10 A.M

Hey GreenFred! Im a garden decorator! Using an old chair to enhances a garden is a good idea. I often place discarded items in the garden. My kids and me collect used coffee cans and make planter's out of them. (You can also use old rain boots or toy wagons for this perpose. Weve also made birdhouses from coffee cans and one gallon milk containers.

Posted by VegFan on June 12, 2012, at 9:36 A,M.

Hello! I have a question for Gardenia. Ive been having a problem rescently with bird's and squirrels' getting into my yard and eating the plants? What can I do to stop them.

THURSDAY　　　　　　　　　　　　　　　Week 26

WATCH FOR

- dates
- time
- parentheses
- run-on sentences

Posted by Gardenia on June 12 2012 at 10 01 a.m.

Hi VegFan. Try hanging shiny objects (such as old CDs or aluminum pie plates around you're yard to scare the animals. The sun light reflecting off this items should sufficiently startel the creetures and make 'em leaf your garden.

Posted by Planty on June, 14 2012 at 5:24 p.M.

I been bothered for years with critters' getting into my garden. One thing that work is soaking some rags in vinigar, and placing the rags around the plant's that the critters like. The smell drive them away sprinkling coffee grounds on the soil has the same effect.

MONDAY   Week 27

Altering the Food Supply

In some area's of the world, people do not have enough

food to survive; the ~~thret~~ *threat* of starvation is always present.

One solution which most certainly is a controversial one is

to grow genetically modified (GM) foods. To develop GM crops,

scientists choose ~~spesific~~ *specific* traits, such as fruit size or disease

~~resistince~~ *resistance*. They ~~identafy~~ *identify* genes (often in ~~a~~ *an* unrelated species)

that control those ~~trates~~ *traits*; then they transfer the ~~jeans~~ *genes* to

another organism. Some people ~~thinks~~ *think* that GM foods are

harmful just because they are ~~artifishul~~ *artificial*. They call them

"Frankenfoods," Referring to the fictitious Dr. Frankenstein.

Error Summary

Capitalization	2
Language Usage	2
Punctuation:	
Apostrophe	1
Comma	3
Parentheses	2
Period	2
Quotation Mark	1
Spelling	7

TUESDAY   Week 27

Scientists have successfully modified rice, corn, and other

kinds of plants. For ~~rezistence~~ *resistance* to insect pests. They ~~acheived~~ *achieved*

this by incorporating a gene from a bacterium called <u>Bacillus</u>

<u>thuringiensis</u>, or <u>Bt</u>. Bt produces a toxin that is used in some

insecticides but that is supposedly safe for humans. Crops

that have the <u>Bt</u> gene don't need as much insecticide to

~~controls~~ *control* pests. This seems better for the environment.

Nevertheless, people who ~~apose~~ *oppose* this use of ~~tecnology~~ *technology* ~~argues~~ *argue*

that <u>Bt</u> harms all insects that come into ~~contack~~ *contact* with the

plants. This includes ~~benifishul~~ *beneficial* insects, such as butterflies

and bees, which pollinate plants.

Error Summary

Capitalization	1
Language Usage	2
Punctuation:	
Apostrophe	1
Comma	5
Period	1
Underlined Words	2
Spelling	6

Name _____

MONDAY   Week 27

EDITING KEY

Altering the Food Supply

In some area's of the world, people do not have enough food to survive, the thret of starvation is always present. One solution which most certainly is a controversial one is to grow genetically modified (GM foods. To develop GM crops, scientists choose spesific traits, such as fruit size or disease resistince. They identafy genes often in a unrelated species) that control those trates; then they transfer the jeans to another organism. Some people thinks that GM foods are harmful just because they are artifishul. They call them "Frankenfoods Referring to the fictitious Dr Frankenstein.

- run-on sentences
- commas
- parentheses
- incomplete sentences
- abbreviations

TUESDAY   Week 27

WATCH FOR

- commas
- incomplete sentences
- scientific names

Scientists have successfully modified rice corn and other kinds of plants. For rezistence to insect pests. They acheived this by incorporating a gene from a bacterium called Bacillus thuringiensis or Bt. Bt produces a toxin that is used in some insecticides but that is supposedly safe for humans. Crops that have the Bt gene dont need as much insecticide to controls pests. This seems better for the environment. Nevertheless people who apose this use of tecnology argues that Bt harms all insects that come into contack with the plants. This includes benifishul insects, such as butterflies and bees which pollinate plants.

WEDNESDAY   Week 27

Another ~~arguemint~~ argument against Frankenfoods, ~~are~~ is that genes can cross ~~acidently~~ accidentally from Modified plant's into non-GM or wild plant species. In fact, this "outcrossing" has ~~happen~~ happened already. In one case, scientists ~~geneticly~~ genetically modified a variety of maize (corn) that farmers grow only as food for livestock. Later, traces of this ~~alterred~~ altered crop was found in a type of maize that farmers grow for people. Outcrossing could be risky. No one knows for sure, though, if any gm foods are completely safe, they could trigger ~~allerjik~~ allergic reactions. There's also the possibility that dna from GM foods could be transferred into human cells after being absorbed by peoples' intestines.

Error Summary

Capitalization	7
Language Usage	2
Punctuation:	
Apostrophe	3
Comma	5
Period	1
Spelling	5

THURSDAY   Week 27

Those in favor of creating Frankenfoods say that the ~~consept~~ concept of modifying foods is not new, they point out that farmers have practiced selective ~~breading~~ breeding for ~~senchuries~~ centuries. Farmers choose plant varieties based on certain, desirable traits, Which isn't much different from what scientists are doing. On the ~~possative~~ positive side, GM technology can provide much larger crop ~~yeilds~~ yields Which means that farmers can feed more people. Foods also can be ~~enjineered~~ engineered to provide a longer shelf life (that is, to make them stay fresh longer) or to be more nutritious. These facts make GM foods, a solution ~~wirth~~ worth considering In a world where people go hungry.

Error Summary

Capitalization	4
Punctuation:	
Apostrophe	1
Comma	4
Period	2
Spelling	7

Name _____

WEDNESDAY   Week 27

Another arguemint against Frankenfoods, are that genes can cross acidently from Modified plant's into non-GM or wild plant species. In fact this "outcrossing" has happen already. In one case, scientists geneticly modified a variety of maize (corn) that farmers grow only as food for livestock. Later traces of this alterred crop was found in a type of maize that farmers grow for people. Outcrossing could be risky. No one knows for sure though if any gm foods are completely safe, they could trigger allerjik reactions. Theres also the possibility that dna from GM foods could be transferred into human cells after being absorbed by peoples' intestines.

- abbreviations
- commas
- run-on sentences
- apostrophes

THURSDAY   Week 27

Those in favor of creating Frankenfoods say that the consept of modifying foods is not new, they point out that farmers have practiced selective breading for senchuries. Farmers choose plant varieties based on certain, desirable traits. Which isnt much different from what scientists are doing. On the possative side, GM technology can provide much larger crop yeilds. Which means that farmers can feed more people. Foods also can be enjineered to provide a longer shelf life (that is, to make them stay fresh longer) or to be more nutritious. These facts make GM foods, a solution wirth considering. In a world where people go hungry.

- run-on sentences
- incomplete sentences
- commas

MONDAY   Week 28

Error Summary

Capitalization	3
Language Usage	2
Punctuation:	
Apostrophe	2
Comma	5
Parentheses	1
Period	1
Question Mark	1
Semicolon	1
Spelling	1

Games with Flying Discs

Are you looking for a fun game that get's you and your friends outdoors, that offers opportunities for exercise and that isnt hard to learn? if so you might try "ultimate" or "disc golf" Each of these games uses a flying disc (also known by the original brand name Frisbee.) Ultimate is a team sport, disc golf is an individual game. Ultimate is similar in some ways to soccer, basketball and american foot ball; In all of these games the players score in the end zone. The rules of ultimate is so simple that players who are unfamiliar with the game can learn it quick.

(editor's marks: get's → gets; isnt → isn't; learn? if → learn? If; "disc golf" → "disc golf."; Frisbee.) → Frisbee).; team sport, → team sport; basketball and → basketball, and; american → American; ball; In → ball. In; is → are; quick → quickly)

TUESDAY   Week 28

Error Summary

Capitalization	2
Language Usage	5
Punctuation:	
Apostrophe	4
Comma	4
Period	2
Semicolon	1
Spelling	5

The playing field for Ultimate is a large, rectangle with two end zones. A reggulation game have two teams of seven players. The object of the game is to throw the disc to a team mate in the opponents end zone. Team member's tosses the disc from player to player as they run, toward the end zone. Once a player catches the disc, him or her must stop and toss it within ten seconds. A player can't run with the disc, if the disc hits the ground or is interrsepted the opposing team gets it. If a player touch another player, the action can be considered a fowl. Notably, there's no referee the players referee themselfs

(editor's marks: reggulation → regulation; have → has; team mate → teammate; opponents → opponent's; member's → member; tosses → toss; him → he; her → she; can't; disc, if → disc. If; interrsepted → intercepted; touch → touches; fowl → foul; there's; referee the → referee; themselfs → themselves)

Name _____

MONDAY   Week 28

- parentheses
- semicolons
- adverbs

Games with Flying Discs

Are you looking for a fun game that get's you and your friends outdoors, that offers opportunities for exercise and that isnt hard to learn. if so you might try "ultimate" or "disc golf" Each of these games uses a flying disc (also known by the original brand name Frisbee.) Ultimate is a team sport, disc golf is an individual game. Ultimate is similar in some ways to soccer basketball and american foot ball; In all of these games the players score in the end zone. The rules of ultimate is so simple that players who are unfamiliar with the game can learn it quick.

TUESDAY   Week 28

- commas
- run-on sentences
- pronouns
- semicolons

The playing field for Ultimate is a large, rectangle with two end zones. A reggulation game have two teams of seven players. The object of the game is to throw the disc to a team mate in the opponents' end zone. Team member's tosses the disc from player to player as they run, toward the end zone. Once a player catches the disc, him or her must stop and toss it within ten seconds. A player cant run with the disc, if the disc hits the ground or is interrsepted the opposing team gets it. If a player touch another player the action can be considered a fowl. Notably, theres no referee the players referee themselfs

WEDNESDAY   Week 28

Like ultimate, disc golf is played [~~playd~~] with a flying disc, or Frisbee. The game has much in common with traditional golf but it requires less [~~fewer~~] equipment [~~ekwipment~~]. In disc golf, you won't need golf balls, clubs or a golf cart. In traditional golf, the object of the game is to get the ball in the hole with the fewest [~~fewer~~] strokes of the golf club. Disc golf's object is the same but the target is usually [~~usual~~] an elevated [~~ellevated~~] metal basket attached to a pole. As the player moves along the fairway, or playing area he [~~him~~] or she [~~her~~] tosses the disc from the spot where the previous toss landed. The course usually includes obstacles such as trees, shrubs and changing landscapes.

Error Summary

Capitalization	1
Language Usage	5
Punctuation:	
Apostrophe	2
Comma	6
Period	1
Spelling	3

THURSDAY   Week 28

Where can you play disc golf or ultimate? Many cities have courses already set up in local parks. In most cases, you don't have to pay anything [~~nothing~~] to play. If your [~~you're~~] city doesn't have such a course you can set up your own in a park or other green space. You wouldn't have to use a [~~no~~] basket on a pole for disc golf; you could use a basket on the ground instead. For a nine-hole disc golf course, you'll need a minimum [~~minamum~~] of about five acres of land. ideally, the course would combine open and wooded areas. The benefits of playing disc golf include [~~includes~~] not only physical conditioning, and aerobic exercise but also the sheer pleasure [~~plezure~~] of the game.

Error Summary

Capitalization	4
Language Usage	3
Punctuation:	
Apostrophe	4
Comma	3
Hyphen	1
Period	3
Question Mark	1
Semicolon	1
Spelling	3

Name _____

WEDNESDAY   Week 28

Like ultimate, disc golf is playd with a flying disc, or Frisbee. The game has much in common with traditional golf but it requires fewer ekwipment. In disc golf, you wont need golf balls, clubs or a golf cart. In traditional golf, the object of the game is to get the ball in the hole with the fewer strokes of the golf club. Disc golfs object is the same but the target is usual an ellevated metal basket attached to a pole. As the player moves along the fairway, or playing area him or her tosses the disc from the spot where the previous toss landed. The course usually includes obstacles. Such as trees shrubs and changing landscapes.

- commas
- words that compare
- pronouns
- adverbs

THURSDAY   Week 28

Where can you play disc golf or ultimate. Many cities have courses already set up in local parks In most cases, you dont have to pay nothing to play. If you're city doesnt have such a course you can set up your own in a park or other Green Space. You wouldnt have to use no basket on a pole for disc golf, you could use a basket on the ground instead. For a nine hole disc golf course youll need a minamum of about five acres of land ideally, the course would combine open and wooded areas. The benefits of playing disc golf includes not only physical conditioning, and Aerobic exercise but also the sheer plezure of the game

- double negatives
- hyphens
- run-on sentences
- semicolons

© Evan-Moor Corp. • EMC 2838 • Daily Paragraph Editing   123

MONDAY   Week 29

Songs of the Whales

The sounds that whales ~~makes~~ make have a musical ~~quallity~~ quality—like songs. Whale songs can be low, soothing, and mysterious, or they can sound light and playful. they are not all alike. Researchers have recorded and ~~analized~~ analyzed thousands of whale songs. And have noticed that these songs ~~varies~~ vary in Pitch and Duration. The songs may be high-pitched or deep; they may be short or long-lasting. Researchers hope to discover the purpose for each type of song and to learn why the songs are so different. Whale songs may even ~~reveel~~ reveal new data about the oceans themselves.

Error Summary

Capitalization	4
Language Usage	2
Punctuation:	
Comma	4
Hyphen	3
Period	2
Spelling	3

TUESDAY   Week 29

If you hear a Humpback whale, You may think you are listening to the cries, moans, roars, and high-pitched ~~squeels~~ squeals of a human. the Blue whale is known for it's ~~distincktive~~ distinctive song, a deep, low call. Toothed whales, such as the killer whale, ~~produces~~ produce a series of whistles, clicks, and groans. ~~Marene~~ Marine scientists are recording whale songs, and posting audio files to the Internet so the songs are ~~accesibbel~~ accessible to the public. People have a an opportunity to listen to the songs and to give feedback. ~~There~~ Their responses help scientists ~~clasify~~ classify the songs and decode them. The online recordings ~~allows~~ allow anyone to hear what ~~this~~ these ocean mammals are saying.

Error Summary

Capitalization	4
Language Usage	4
Punctuation:	
Apostrophe	1
Comma	7
Dash	1
Hyphen	1
Spelling	6

Name _____

MONDAY   Week 29

• verbs
• commas
• hyphens

Songs of the Whales

The sounds that whales makes have a musical quallity—like songs. Whale songs can be low soothing and mysterious or they can sound light and playful. they are not all alike. Researchers have recorded and analized thousands of whale songs. And have noticed that these songs varies in Pitch and Duration. The songs may be high-pitched or deep; they may be short or long lasting. Researchers hope to discover the purpose for each type-of-song, and to learn why the songs are so different. Whale songs may even reveel new data about the oceans themselves

TUESDAY   Week 29

• incomplete sentences
• hyphens
• dashes

If you hear a Humpback whale. You may think you are listening to the cries moans roars and high pitched squeels of a human. the Blue whale is known for it's distincktive song a deep, low call. Toothed whales, such as the killer whale, produces a series of whistles clicks and groans. Marene scientists are recording whale songs, and posting audio files to the Internet so the songs are accesibbel to the public. People have a opportunity to listen to the songs and to give feedback. There responses help scientists clasify the songs and decode them. The online recordings allows anyone to hear what this ocean mammals are saying.

WEDNESDAY   Week 29

Marine scientists know that whales make sounds for different reasons. Toothed whales for example make sounds primarily to orient ~~theirselves~~ themselves in the ocean the whales release sounds and ~~listens~~ listen for the ~~echos~~ echoes which tell them where objects are located. This process called echolocation is useful to toothed whales in the same way that ~~eye site~~ eyesight is useful to humans. Baleen whales (those that do not have ~~tooths~~ teeth, such as humpback whales) use sounds to ~~attracts~~ attract mates and to ~~allert~~ alert other whales to food sources and danger. A change in a particular whale song over time could indicate that ocean conditions are changing (which ~~obvious~~ obviously would affect people).

Error Summary

Capitalization	1
Language Usage	5
Punctuation:	
Comma	5
Parentheses	2
Period	1
Spelling	3

THURSDAY   Week 29

After analyzing thousands of blue whale song ~~rikordings~~ recordings marine scientists have found that the songs are getting lower in pitch every year. Why is this happening? Maybe the whales need to use different ~~frequencys~~ frequencies to communicate because, the oceans are getting ~~crowdeder~~ more crowded with ships. (Lower sounds can travel ~~more far then~~ farther than high-pitched sounds.) Or, maybe the change in pitch is ~~do~~ due to ocean pollution. Or to an evolution in mating rituals. Researchers are ~~considdering~~ considering various ~~theorys~~ theories. With the publics help in cataloging and ~~decodeing~~ decoding the recorded whale songs researchers may one day find the answer to this mystery.

Error Summary

Capitalization	1
Language Usage	4
Punctuation:	
Apostrophe	1
Comma	4
Parentheses	1
Period	1
Question Mark	1
Spelling	6

WEDNESDAY   Week 29

Marine scientists know that whales make sounds for different reasons. Toothed whales for example make sounds primarily to orient theirselves in the ocean the whales release sounds and listens for the echos which tell them where objects are located. This process called echolocation is useful to toothed whales in the same way that eye site is useful to humans. Baleen whales (those that do not have tooths, such as humpback whales use sounds to attracts mates and to allert other whales to food sources and danger. A change in a particular whale song over time could indicate that ocean conditions are changing (which obvious would affect people.

- pronouns
- commas
- compound words
- adverbs

THURSDAY   Week 29

After analyzing thousands of blue whale song rikordings marine scientists have found that the songs are getting lower in pitch every year. Why is this happening. Maybe the whales need to use different frequencys to communicate because, the oceans are getting crowdeder with ships. (Lower sounds can travel more far then high-pitched sounds). Or, maybe the change in pitch is do to ocean pollution. Or to a evolution in mating rituals. Researchers are considdering various theorys. With the publics help in cataloging and decodeing the recorded whale songs researchers may one day find the answer to this mystery.

- hyphens
- words that compare
- punctuation with parentheses
- incomplete sentences

MONDAY   Week 30

Peer Mediation Program

Date: ~~o~~ctober 17, 2011

To: ~~m~~r~~.~~ ~~v~~assiliou, ~~s~~chool principal

From: Guadalupe V., ~~j~~oshua R., ~~n~~ina ~~m~~.

Subject: Proposal for a peer mediation ~~progrram~~ (program) at school

Project ~~Descripshun~~ (Description): Student conflicts ~~occurs~~ (occur) daily in middle school~~,~~. peer ~~medeation~~ (mediation) is a ~~prosess~~ (process) that ~~let~~ (lets) students who have conflicts with each other meet face to face to ~~discus~~ (discuss) ~~confidenshul~~ (confidential) issues in front of a trained mediator. The mediator enforces fair ~~prosedures~~ (procedures) and ~~resolve~~ (resolves) conflict. Teachers will ~~elekt~~ (elect) students to serve as mediators.

Error Summary

Capitalization	9
Language Usage	3
Punctuation:	
Comma	1
Period	4
Spelling	8

TUESDAY   Week 30

What We ~~need~~ (Need): To start with, we need a list of criteria for ~~chosing~~ (choosing) eligible students to become peer mediators. Teachers will elect ~~cannidates~~ (candidates) based on ~~this~~ (these) criteria. We also need criteria to determine—on a case-by-case basis—whether peer mediation is ~~aproprieut~~ (appropriate). We need clear procedures for ~~runing~~ (running) the sessions consistently. Once a procedure is developed and mediators are ~~chose~~ (chosen), the mediators should practice the ~~procejure~~ (procedure). The only materials needed ~~is~~ (are) a printer and paper so we can make confidentiality ~~agreemense~~ (agreements) which ~~partisipents~~ (participants) (including mediators) will sign. Finally, the program needs to have a location to conduct mediation ~~sessiones~~ (sessions) at school.

Error Summary

Capitalization	1
Language Usage	3
Punctuation:	
Comma	1
Dash	1
Hyphen	1
Parentheses	1
Spelling	8

Name _____

Peer Mediation Program

Date: october 17 2011

To: mr vassiliou, school principal

From: Guadalupe V., joshua R., nina m

Subject: Proposal for a peer mediation progrram at school

Project Descripshun: Student conflicts occurs daily in middle school, peer medeation is a prosess that let students who have conflicts with each other meet face to face to discus confidenshul issues in front of a trained mediator. The mediator enforces fair prosedures and resolve conflict. Teachers will elekt students to serve as mediators

• dates
• names and titles of people
• abbreviations
• run-on sentences

What We need: To start with, we need a list of criteria for chosing eligible students to become peer mediators. Teachers will elect cannidates based on this criteria. We also need criteria to determine—on a case-by case basis whether peer mediation is aproprieut. We need clear procedures for runing the sessions consistently. Once a procedure is developed and mediators are chose, the mediators should practice the procejure. The only materials needed is a printer and paper so we can make confidentiality agreemense which partisipents (including mediators will sign. Finally, the program needs to have a location to conduct mediation sessiones at school.

• dashes
• adjectives
• hyphens
• parentheses

WEDNESDAY   Week 30

What peer mediators will do: a peer mediators job is to remain neutral, to ensure that both participants can explain their sides of the dispute without ~~no~~ *any* interruption, and ~~presenting~~ *to present* potential ~~salutions~~ *solutions* to the problem. At the start of each ~~seshun~~ *session*, the mediator will shake hand's with both participants to show neutrality During the session each participant will have ~~a~~ *an* uninterrupted period of time To respond to the other persons ~~statemints~~ *statements*. The mediator will take notes enforce the rules and follow up with questions or comments to clear up any misunderstandings. Finally, everyone in the session will ~~proppose~~ *propose* solutions to the problem.

Error Summary
Capitalization	6
Language Usage	2
Punctuation:	
Apostrophe	3
Comma	3
Period	2
Sentence Structure	1
Spelling	4

THURSDAY   Week 30

Outcome: At the end of the school year We will take a ~~survay~~ *survey* of all students who participated in peer mediation, to see if the program helped with ~~there~~ *their* situations. If we receive positive feed back from the majority of those students we will plan on continuing the program in future years. However if most of the ~~responces~~ *responses* are ~~negetive~~ *negative*, we will discontinue the program Or evaluate how to improve it

Conflict can affect student's success and ~~happyness~~ *happiness*, and it is ~~preferible~~ *preferable* to resolve any conflicts ~~quick~~ *quickly*. We hope you will approve our ~~proposil~~ *proposal* For a peer mediation program at ~~are~~ *our* school.

Error Summary
Capitalization	3
Language Usage	1
Punctuation:	
Apostrophe	1
Comma	5
Period	3
Spelling	9

WEDNESDAY   Week 30

What peer mediators will do: a peer mediators job is to remain neutral, to ensure that both participants can explain their sides of the dispute without no interruption, and presenting potential salutions to the problem. At the start of each seshun, the mediator will shake hand's with both participants to show neutrality During the session each participant will have a uninterrupted period of time. To respond to the other persons statemints. The mediator will take notes enforce the rules and follow up with questions or comments to clear up any misunderstandings. Finally, everyone in the session will proppose solutions to the problem.

- parallel structure
- double negatives
- commas
- incomplete sentences

THURSDAY   Week 30

Outcome: At the end of the school year. We will take a survay of all students, who participated in peer mediation, to see if the program helped with there situations. If we receive positive feed back from the majority of those students we will plan on continuing the program in future years. However if most of the responces are negetive, we will discontinue the program. Or evaluate how to improve it

　　　Conflict can affect student's success, and happyness, and it is preferible to resolve any conflicts quick. We hope you will approve our proposil. For a peer mediation program at are school.

- incomplete sentences
- adverbs
- adjectives
- apostrophes

MONDAY   Week 31

Tree-Climbing Goats

Morocco is a dry mountainous country in northwestern africa. Along the coast is an harsh rugged area, that is home to large forests of argan trees. It's the only place in the world, where these gnarled thorny trees grow wild. The trees bloom in april but their fruit (olive-like berries) takes more than a year to mature and rippen. Tamri goats, native to this area, enjoy snacking on the berries. Like sure-footed acrobats, the large goats scale the trees and ballance on the narrow branches as they feasts on the leafs and berries. Yes these ennergetic goats actually climb trees!

Editing marks above text: a (over "an harsh"), ripen (over "rippen"), balance (over "ballance"), feast (over "feasts"), leaves (over "leafs"), energetic (over "ennergetic")

Error Summary

Capitalization	2
Language Usage	2
Punctuation:	
Apostrophe	1
Comma	8
Hyphen	2
Parentheses	1
Spelling	4

TUESDAY   Week 31

The Tamri goats habit of climbing argan trees make them unusual. But what gives the goats this special skill and makes them so sure-footed and agile; Their split hoofs are the secret to they're climbing skills. Two toes on each foot spread out And allow for greater mobility. The soft bendable tissue between the toes enable the goats to grip the branches—Similar to the way that human hands grasp. The goats also have dewclaws which are claw-like toes higher up on the animals legs. (Dogs and cats also have dewclaws. These strong tough toes help the goats pull theirselves up onto the tree branches And balence on the slender limbs.

Editing marks above text: makes (over "make"), their (over "they're"), enables (over "enable"), themselves (over "theirselves"), balance (over "balence")

Error Summary

Capitalization	3
Language Usage	3
Punctuation:	
Apostrophe	3
Comma	3
Hyphen	1
Parentheses	1
Period	2
Question Mark	1
Spelling	2

MONDAY   Week 31

Tree-Climbing Goats

Morocco is a dry mountainous country in northwestern africa. Along the coast is an harsh rugged area, that is home to large forests of argan trees. Its the only place in the world, where these gnarled thorny trees grow wild. The trees bloom in april but their fruit (olive like berries takes more than a year to mature and rippen. Tamri goats, native to this area, enjoy snacking on the berries. Like sure footed acrobats the large goats scale the trees and ballance on the narrow branches as they feasts on the leafs and berries. Yes these ennergetic goats actually climb trees!

- commas
- parentheses
- hyphens

TUESDAY   Week 31

The Tamri goats habit of climbing argan trees make them unusual. But what gives the goats this special skill and makes them so sure-footed and agile. Their split hoofs' are the secret to they're climbing skills. Two toes on each foot spread out. And allow for greater mobility. The soft bendable tissue between the toes enable the goats to grip the branches—Similar to the way that human hands grasp. The goats also have dewclaws which are claw like toes higher up on the animals legs. (Dogs and cats also have dewclaws). These strong tough toes help the goats pull theirselves up onto the tree branches. And balence on the slender limbs.

- verbs
- apostrophes
- incomplete sentences
- punctuation with parentheses

WEDNESDAY   Week 31

Once they are eaten the tasty argan berries ~~passes~~ **pass**
through the goats' digestive systems. The goats can ~~dijest~~ **digest** the
fruit, but not the hard nut inside the fruit. Consequently the
nuts are released whole from the goats' bodies. Moroccan
farmers ~~rummidge~~ **rummage** through the goat droppings to collect the
hard-shelled nuts. Inside each nut are one to three seeds
which ~~is~~ **are** ground to produce a ~~valuble~~ **valuable** oil. Argan oil is so
prized that moroccan farmers don't want to waste any seeds
which is why they ~~retreive~~ **retrieve** them from goat droppings. The oil
is nutritious and has many uses. It is added to foods, body
lotions, soaps, and ~~people also use it in~~ cosmetics.

Error Summary

Capitalization	1
Language Usage	2
Punctuation:	
Apostrophe	2
Comma	5
Hyphen	1
Sentence Structure	1
Spelling	4

THURSDAY   Week 31

~~Deemand~~ **Demand** for argan oil ~~have~~ **has** caused some concern for
the future of the forests; the forests have ~~deacresed~~ **decreased** by
30 percent in a 100-year period. Overgrazing by goats and
~~agresive~~ **aggressive** harvesting by farmers ~~is~~ **are** two contributing ~~faktors~~ **factors**.

Argan trees and wild goats have shared this region of
coastal morocco for centuries; both have adapted to the
regions' harsh, arid climate. Although goats are adaptable
animals in general, Nowhere else on the planet do they
habitually climb trees. A tree full of scruffy goats—as many
as 15 at a time—~~are~~ **is** a ~~hillarious~~ **hilarious** sight. Conservationists are
doing their part to ensure that the tradition continues.

Error Summary

Capitalization	3
Language Usage	3
Punctuation:	
Apostrophe	1
Comma	2
Dash	1
Hyphen	1
Period	3
Spelling	5

WEDNESDAY   Week 31

Once they are eaten the tasty argan berries passes through the goats digestive systems. The goats can dijest the fruit, but not the hard nut inside the fruit. Consequently the nuts are released whole from the goats' bodies. Moroccan farmers rummidge through the goat droppings to collect the hard shelled nuts. Inside each nut are one to three seeds which is ground to produce a valuble oil. Argan oil is so prized that moroccan farmers dont want to waste any seeds which is why they retreive them from goat droppings. The oil is nutritious and has many uses. It is added to foods, body lotions, soaps, and people also use it in cosmetics.

- verbs
- commas
- hyphens
- parallel structure

THURSDAY   Week 31

Deemand for argan oil have caused some concern for the future of the forests; the forests have deacresed by 30 percent in a 100 year period. Overgrazing by goats and agresive harvesting by farmers is two contributing faktors

Argan trees and wild goats have shared this region of coastal morocco for centuries, both have adapted to the regions' harsh arid climate. Although goats are adaptable animals in general. Nowhere else on the planet do they habitually climb trees. A tree full of scruffy goats as many as 15 at a time—are a hillarious sight. Conservationists are doing their part to ensure that the tradition continues

- place names
- run-on sentences
- hyphens
- dashes

MONDAY   Week 32

Without a Home

I'll never forget the day that dad ~~losed~~ *lost* his job. He had worked at the steel mill for twenty-five years. Although he didn't ~~completely~~ *completely* claim to enjoy his job, the ~~sallery~~ *salary* was ~~desent~~ *decent*. But the mill was shutting down, leaving many people without ~~no~~ jobs. Dad announced the news one ~~evning~~ *evening* after dinner, when we were still at the table chatting about trifling things. He told us we'd have to "tighten our belts," by which he meant that we needed to be less extravagant. I ~~inturprited~~ *interpreted* it literally, ~~pitchering~~ *picturing* our belts getting tighter. "Don't worry," Dad reassured us. "We won't be homeless."

Error Summary

Capitalization	2
Language Usage	2
Punctuation:	
Apostrophe	3
Hyphen	1
Quotation Mark	3
Sentence Structure	1
Spelling	5

TUESDAY   Week 32

I ~~acompaneed~~ *accompanied* Dad the first time he went to the office at the department of workforce development, then we drove out to the lake to cheer ~~ourselfs~~ *ourselves* up. We went fishing for a couple hours, but didn't catch ~~nothing~~ *anything*. Still, we had fun. After packing up the fishing poles, bait, and tackle box, we headed home. That's when the day turned sour. Traveling home, Dad ~~misjuged~~ *misjudged* the size of a rock in the road. Our old station wagon hit it and immediately started making ~~an horid~~ *a horrid* noise. The exhaust system had ~~fell~~ *fallen* apart and was leaking, but it sounded much ~~worst~~ *worse* than it was. Dad tied the ~~broke~~ *broken* pieces together with wire, and duct tape. Then we continued home.

Error Summary

Capitalization	6
Language Usage	5
Punctuation:	
Apostrophe	2
Comma	5
Period	1
Spelling	4

| MONDAY | Week 32 |

Without a Home

I'll never forget the day that dad losed his job. He had worked at the steel mill for twenty five years. Although he didnt completely claim to enjoy his job, the sallery was desent. But the mill was shutting down, leaving many people without no jobs. Dad announced the news one evning after dinner, when we were still at the table chatting about trifling things. He told us wed have to "tighten our belts, by which he meant that we needed to be less extravagant. I inturprited it literally, pitchering our belts getting tighter. "Don't worry, Dad reassured us. "we wont be homeless.

- misplaced modifiers
- double negatives
- quotation marks

| TUESDAY | Week 32 |

I acompaneed Dad the first time he went to the office at the department of workforce development, then we drove out to the Lake to cheer ourselfs up. We went fishing for a couple hours, but didnt catch nothing. still, we had fun. After packing up the fishing poles bait and tackle box, we headed home. Thats when the day turned sour. Traveling home Dad misjuged the size of a rock in the road. Our old station wagon hit it and immediately started making an horid noise. The exhaust system had fell apart and was leaking, but it sounded much worst than it was. Dad tied the broke pieces together with wire, and duct tape. Then we continued home.

- names of organizations
- run-on sentences
- words that compare

WEDNESDAY   Week 32

Error Summary

Capitalization	4
Language Usage	4
Punctuation:	
Apostrophe	1
Comma	4
Period	1
Quotation Mark	2
Spelling	3

The next day, Mom took the station wagon down to the auto repair shop to get an ~~estamite~~ *estimate* for fixing the ~~exaust~~ *exhaust* leak. ~~A~~ *An* hour later, the car pulled up in front of the house and the door slammed shut. When dad asked how much the repair was ~~gonna~~ *going to* cost mom sighed and responded, "Too much."

"Ugh" Dad uttered softly. then we'll have to wait until next month, he added. So the car sat in front of the house and got ~~dustyer~~ *dustier*, and leaves collected around the tires.

Almost two months later Dad started up the cars engine and brushed away the dust. ~~Him~~ *He* and ~~me~~ *I* headed off to get the car fixed . . . finally.

THURSDAY   Week 32

Error Summary

Capitalization	4
Language Usage	2
Punctuation:	
Apostrophe	2
Comma	5
Exclamation Point	1
Hyphen	1
Period	1
Quotation Mark	1
Spelling	4

We had just ~~drove~~ *driven* past the old Steel Mill when Dads wire-and-tape repair broke. The car sounded like a jackhammer in a closet full of thick winter coats. Dad pulled over stopped and walked to the back of the car. After a few minutes, we heard a ~~mufled~~ *muffled* crying sound near the front of the car. We popped the hood open and looked ~~aggast~~ *aghast* As a dirty stiff-tailed animal dropped down from the engine.

"Good grief! Its *an* a opossum! exclaimed dad. The animal had been living under the hood of the car for two months. Dazed from the noise it waddled away and ~~vannished~~ *vanished* beneath some shrubs. The opossum was homeless now and I felt ~~giulty~~ *guilty*.

WEDNESDAY   Week 32

- verbs
- quotation marks
- pronouns

The next day, Mom took the station wagon down to the auto repair shop to get an estamite. For fixing the exaust leak. A hour later, the car pulled up in front of the house and the door slammed shut. When dad asked how much the repair was gonna cost mom sighed and responded, "Too much."

"Ugh" Dad uttered softly. then we'll have to wait until next month", he added. So the car sat in front of the house and got dustyer, and leaves collected around the tires.

Almost two months later Dad started up the cars engine and brushed away the dust. Him and me headed off to get the car fixed . . . finally.

THURSDAY   Week 32

- end punctuation
- quotation marks

We had just drove past the old Steel Mill when Dads wire-and-tape repair broke. The car sounded like a jackhammer in a closet full of thick winter coats. Dad pulled over stopped and walked to the back of the car. After a few minutes, we heard a mufled crying sound near the front of the car. We popped the hood open and looked aggast. As a dirty stiff tailed animal dropped down from the engine.

"Good grief Its a opossum! exclaimed dad. The animal had been living under the hood of the car for two months. Dazed from the noise it waddled away and vannished beneath some shrubs. The opossum was homeless now and I felt giulty.

MONDAY Week 33

Meeting with a School Counselor

"Hi Mr Moore. My Mom said I have to come and talk
with you about my ~~skedule~~ *schedule* for next semester."

"Good morning Deeandra. Please take a seat"

"I know what changes Id like to make next semester
but mom and ~~me~~ *I* dont agree on what classes I should take.
I just think its totally not her ~~bizness~~ *business*."

"well deeandra I happen to ~~agreed~~ *agree* with you you have
the right to tailor your schedule to your interests, but with
that right comes responsibility."

"Whatever mr. Moore. I just want to get this done."

Error Summary

Capitalization	6
Language Usage	2
Punctuation:	
Apostrophe	3
Comma	6
Period	3
Quotation Mark	3
Spelling	2

TUESDAY Week 33

"So, deeandra what classes would you like to take next
semester? We'll see if the changes ~~is~~ *are* manageable."

"Um for sure I want to drop Algebra. Im ~~desprit~~ *desperate* to
get out of that class!"

"Hmm I see. I can tell you quite positively that you
cant drop that class you wont be ~~elajible~~ *eligible* to graduate without
~~them~~ *it*. Some classes are compulsory for all students"

"Oh, phooey!"

"Is there another change youre thinking about?"

"Yeah I want another study hall every day."

"I'll ~~prints~~ *print* out your schedule so we can ~~glanse~~ *glance* at it.

Error Summary

Capitalization	2
Language Usage	3
Punctuation:	
Apostrophe	4
Comma	4
Exclamation Point	1
Period	2
Question Mark	2
Quotation Mark	3
Spelling	3

MONDAY	Week 33

Meeting with a School Counselor

"Hi Mr Moore. My Mom said I have to come and talk with you about my skedule for next semester."

"Good morning Deeandra. Please take a seat

"I know what changes Id like to make next semester but mom and me dont agree on what classes I should take. I just think its totally not her bizness."

"well deeandra I happen to agreed with you, you have the right to tailor your schedule to your interests, but with that right comes responsibility."

Whatever mr. Moore. I just want to get this done.

- dialogue
- personal names
- titles of people
- verbs

TUESDAY	Week 33

"So, deeandra what classes would you like to take next semester. We'll see if the changes is manageable."

"Um for sure I want to drop Algebra. Im desprit to get out of that class!"

Hmm I see. I can tell you quite positively that you cant drop that class you wont be elajible to graduate without them. Some classes are compulsory for all students"

"Oh, phooey

"Is there another change youre thinking about."

"Yeah I want another study hall every day."

"I'll prints out your schedule so we can glanse at it.

- pronouns
- personal names
- apostrophes
- end punctuation

WEDNESDAY　　　　　　　　　　　　　Week 33

"Ah Im a little puzzled about why youd like to add
                                    hall
another study haul deeandra. You already have two of them
            schedule
in your schejool. You have a lunch period besides, and the
                                academic
rest of your day is taken up with accademic classes all of
                                graduate
which are required in order for you to grajuate."

"But I thought we were allowed to have up to three study
                                    allowed
                                    only
halls, mr. Moore. I only have two study halls."

"Thats true. My point is that the only way we could
add a study hall to your schedule Is if we fill your lunch
period I don't see why you'd want to do that. Say couldnt I
                                foreign
interest you in a foren language class or a computer class"

Error Summary

Capitalization	3
Language Usage	1
Punctuation:	
Apostrophe	4
Comma	4
Period	2
Question Mark	1
Quotation Mark	1
Sentence Structure	1
Spelling	5

THURSDAY　　　　　　　　　　　　　Week 33

                                            were
"Come on, Mr moore! You said that my classes was up
to me what I want is another study hall"
                                decision
"Well, I can't say that I care for your desision to
                            you're
discard a lunch period but your right about the rules?"
                            quit
"One more thing, mr Moore. I want to quite the debate
                        choral
club after school and join the coral group instead debate is
too
to much work I dont like it anymore."
                        calendar
"Im looking at the callendar Deeandra. Lets see. You
could quit the debate club or belong to both clubs. With the
music concert coming up the choral group is a great choice!"

"Uh on second thought, forget it."

Error Summary

Capitalization	4
Language Usage	1
Punctuation:	
Apostrophe	3
Comma	4
Period	7
Quotation Mark	2
Spelling	6

WEDNESDAY   Week 33

"Ah Im a little puzzled about why youd like to add another study haul deeandra. You already have two of them in your schejool. You have a lunch period besides, and the rest of your day is taken up with accademic classes all of which are required in order for you to grajuate."

But I thought we were allow to have up to three study halls, mr. Moore. I only have two study halls."

"Thats true. My point is that the only way we could add a study hall to your schedule. Is if we fill your lunch period, I don't see why you'd want to do that. Say couldnt I interest you in a foren language class or a computer class"

- commas
- incomplete sentences
- misplaced modifiers

THURSDAY   Week 33

"Come on, Mr moore! You said that my classes was up to me, what I want is another study hall

"Well, I can't say that I care for your desision to discard a lunch period but your right about the rules?"

"One more thing, mr Moore. I want to quite the debate club after school and join the coral group instead debate is to much work I dont like it anymore."

"Im looking at the callendar Deeandra. Lets see. You could quit the debate club or belong to both clubs. With the music concert coming up the choral group is a great choice!

"Uh on second thought, forget it."

- dialogue
- end punctuation
- titles of people

MONDAY   Week 34

A Challenge for Animators

One challenge that animators face when creating movies, video games and cartoons is deciding how realistic to make the characters. this is tricky because of a phenomenon called the "uncanny valley." Basically, people have positive emotional responses toward objects that resemble us—but only up to a point. If objects seem too human, viewers find them strange and creepy, or uncanny. (the "valley" of the uncanny valley is literally the dip in the line graph that plots viewer responses to the relative humanness of traits portrayed.) most animators try to avoid the uncanny valley.

Error Summary
Capitalization	3
Language Usage	3
Punctuation:	
Comma	3
Parentheses	1
Period	4
Spelling	4

TUESDAY   Week 34

Ironically, most audiences want to see realism in animated movies and games as long as the animations are not supposed to be scary. Animators take pride in achieving more, and more realistic effects. In fact, realism often is a selling point. companies advertise it to attract larger audiences. So how can game designers and filmmakers respect the critical limit for realism? In other words, how can they avoid the creepy factor as they develop animated games and films? One solution is to focus on making environments (such as scenery, buildings and weather) realistic rather than making the characters themselves seem like real people.

Error Summary
Capitalization	1
Language Usage	3
Punctuation:	
Comma	3
Parentheses	1
Period	2
Question Mark	2
Spelling	6

Name _____

A Challenge for Animators

One challenge that animators face. when creating movies video games and cartoons is deciding how realistic to make the characters this is tricky because of a phenomenon called the "uncanny valley" Basickly, people have positive emoshional responses toward objects that resembles us—but only up to a point. If objects seem too human viewers finds them strange and creepy, or uncanny. (the "valley" of the uncanny valley is litterally the dip in the line graph that plots viewer responses to the rellative humanness of traits portrayed). most animators tries to avoid the uncanny valley

WATCH FOR

- run-on sentences
- incomplete sentences
- punctuation with quotation marks
- punctuation with parentheses

Ironically, most audiences wants to see realism in animated movies and games as long as the animations are not supposed to be scary. Animators takes pride in acheiving more, and more realistic effects. In fact, realism often is a selling point companies advertise. it to atract larger audienses. So how can game designers and filmmakers respect the critikal limit for realism In other words, how can they avoid the creepy facter as they develops animated games and films One solution is to focus on making environments, (such as scenery, buildings, and weather) realistic rather than making the characters themselfs seem like real people

WATCH FOR

- verbs
- commas
- end punctuation

WEDNESDAY　　　　　　　　　　Week 34

for some audiences, realism ~~defeat~~ *defeats* the purpose of animation; watching animated movies ~~offer a~~ *offers an* escape from reality for a while. Characters such as the Parr ~~f~~Family in the movie The ~~incredibles~~ or the kids in the long-running ~~tv~~ series The ~~simpsons~~ are fun to watch. We can relate to them because they are moderately humanlike but not ~~total~~ *totally* realistic. Moreover, animated characters can do ~~outragous~~ *outrageous* things that ~~is~~ *are* impossible in reality. For example, Bob Parr (~~mr~~ Incredible) escapes his ~~rooteen~~ *routine* life once a week to fight crime as a superhero. we enjoy these stories because the characters ~~bare~~ *bear* only a slight resemblance to real people.

Error Summary
Capitalization	8
Language Usage	5
Punctuation:	
Comma	2
Hyphen	1
Parentheses	1
Period	2
Underlined Words	2
Spelling	3

THURSDAY　　　　　　　　　　Week 34

On the other hand, realistic animation—especially in video games ~~enhance~~ *enhances* a viewers experience. Realistic ~~visial~~ *visual* details ~~is~~ *are* more exciting for ~~g~~Gamers. When the characters appear lifelike, though, their movements and expressions must also be natural. the characters must appear to stand, run, breathe, speak, and interact with each other just as real humans do. If the animator ~~miss~~ *misses* a detail, such as matching characters' lip movement with their speech, the characters ~~seems~~ *seem* creepy. Or if the background is flat and shallow instead of three-dimensional, the actions can be ~~dissturbing~~ *disturbing*. To avoid the uncanny valley, ~~animaters~~ *animators* may use less realism.

Error Summary
Capitalization	2
Language Usage	4
Punctuation:	
Apostrophe	2
Comma	7
Dash	1
Hyphen	1
Period	1
Spelling	3

WEDNESDAY   Week 34

for some audiences, realism defeat the purpose of animation; watching animated movies offer a escape from reality for a while. Characters such as the Parr Family in the movie The incredibles or the kids in the long running tv series <u>The</u> <u>simpsons</u> are fun to watch. We can relate to them because they are moderately humanlike but not total realistic. Moreover animated characters can do outragous things that is impossible in reality. For example Bob Parr (mr Incredible escapes his rooteen life once a week to fight crime as a superhero we enjoy these stories because the characters bare only a slight resemblance to real people.

- run-on sentences
- movie titles
- hyphens
- adverbs

THURSDAY   Week 34

On the other hand, realistic animation—especially in video games enhance a viewers experience. Realistic visial details is more exciting for Gamers. When the characters appear lifelike though their movements and expressions must also be natural. the characters must appear to stand run breathe speak and interact with each other just as real humans do If the animator miss a detail, such as matching characters lip movement with their speech; the characters seems creepy. Or if the background is flat and shallow instead of three dimensional, the actions can be dissturbing. To avoid the uncanny valley, animaters may use less realism.

- verbs
- dashes
- hyphens

MONDAY   Week 35

A Generous Visitor

A peculiar-looking man knocked on the door of the rustic ~~russtic~~ log cabin. Eight-year-old Cora opened the door and gasped, for the man looked like no one she had ever seen ~~saw~~ before. He wore a large burlap sack that had once been filled with coffee beans. There were ~~was~~ holes cut out for his head, arms, and ~~two holes for his~~ legs. A rope served as a belt. He didn't wear ~~no~~ shoes yet snow still covered ~~coverd~~ the ground. a tin cooking pot sat on his head.

"Mama"! called cora. "Could you come quickly, I think this man is in need of help."

Error Summary

Capitalization	2
Language Usage	3
Punctuation:	
Comma	1
Hyphen	3
Period	1
Question Mark	1
Quotation Mark	3
Sentence Structure	1
Spelling	2

TUESDAY   Week 35

Martha had gone ~~went~~ into the loft to fetch a blanket that needed mending but she could hear the visitor. "No, child," he said to Cora. "I don't need help. I'm here to help your family."

By then, Martha had climbed ~~climed~~ down the ladder and come ~~came~~ to the door. "My husband is out in the barn taking care of the cows," she said to the stranger. "If you go back there ~~their~~ to see him, he will show you where you can sleep for a few days. Meanwhile, I'll dish up some squirrel stew for you."

"Thank you all the same, Ma'am, but I'm not hungry. Anyway, I do not eat meat, and I prefer to sleep under the stars," he replied ~~replyd~~ in a soothing cordial ~~corgial~~ tone.

Error Summary

Language Usage	2
Punctuation:	
Apostrophe	2
Comma	8
Quotation Mark	6
Spelling	4

Name _____

- hyphens
- parallel structure
- dialogue

A Generous Visitor

A peculiar looking man knocked on the door of the russtic log cabin. Eight year old Cora opened the door and gasped, for the man looked like no one she had ever saw before. He wore a large burlap sack that had once been filled with coffee beans. There was holes cut out for his head, arms, and two holes for his legs. A rope served as a belt. He didn't wear no shoes yet snow still coverd the ground, a tin cooking pot sat on his head.

"Mama"! called cora. Could you come quickly. I think this man is in need of help.

- verbs
- commas
- dialogue
- apostrophes

Martha had went into the loft to fetch a blanket that needed mending but she could hear the visitor. "No, child, he said to Cora. I don't need help. I'm here to help your family.

By then Martha had climed down the ladder and came to the door. "My husband is out in the barn taking care of the cows she said to the stranger. "If you go back their to see him, he will show you where you can sleep for a few days. Meanwhile, Ill dish up some squirrel stew for you.

"Thank you all the same Ma'am but Im not hungry. Anyway, I do not eat meat and I prefer to sleep under the stars he replyd in a soothing corgial tone.

WEDNESDAY   Week 35

"Well, then," said martha, "why have you come?"

The unusual visitor explained that he had two gift's for the fronteer [frontier] family. "I have some apple trees—really, theyre only saplings—and a horse. You may have them. Ill help you plant the saplings; the horse will be helpful on your farm."

Martha and Cora was [were] confused. They wondered how this pawper [pauper] could afford to be so generous. "Run and get Papa," Martha told Cora who hurryed [hurried] to the barn.

When Clarence saw the stranger, he said, "You must be johnny appleseed. I heard about you when last I was in town. From peoples' description, Id reconize [recognize] you anywhere."

Error Summary

Capitalization	4
Language Usage	1
Punctuation:	
Apostrophe	5
Comma	2
Period	1
Question Mark	1
Quotation Mark	6
Spelling	4

THURSDAY   Week 35

johnny laughed. "I know I look different from others but my attire and my way of life suits [suit] me" he explained.

Clarence nodded. "I heard that you bought that horse from the Smith family, mr appleseed and that it was lame. did you really buy a piece of land so the horse could graze while recovering. Why dont you keep the horse for your self?

"I don't need a horse but I can see that you do. Besides my apple business keeps me on the move. Wont you help me out by giving this horse a home?"

Clarence gladly accepted. Years later, the family was still talking about their soupurb [superb] good fortune.

Error Summary

Capitalization	4
Language Usage	1
Punctuation:	
Apostrophe	2
Comma	5
Period	2
Question Mark	2
Quotation Mark	4
Spelling	2

WEDNESDAY   Week 35

Well, then, said martha, why have you come.

The unusual visitor explained that he had two gift's for the fronteer family. "I have some apple trees—really, theyre only saplings—and a horse. You may have them. Ill help you plant the saplings, the horse will be helpful on your farm.

Martha and Cora was confused. They wondered how this pawper could afford to be so generous. "Run and get Papa," Martha told Cora who hurryed to the barn.

When Clarence saw the stranger, he said "You must be johnny appleseed. I heard about you when last I was in town. From peoples' description, Id reconize you anywhere.

- dialogue
- apostrophes

THURSDAY   Week 35

johnny laughed. I know I look different from others but my attire and my way of life suits me he explained.

Clarence nodded. "I heard that you bought that horse from the Smith family, mr appleseed and that it was lame? did you really buy a piece of land so the horse could graze while recovering. Why dont you keep the horse for your self?

"I don't need a horse but I can see that you do. Besides my apple business keeps me on the move. Wont you help me out by giving this horse a home

Clarence gladly accepted. Years later, the family was still talking about their soupurb good fortune.

- dialogue
- abbreviations
- end punctuation

MONDAY   Week 36

Empty Bowls

According to the United Nations' Committee on World Food Security, nearly one out of every six people in the world, thats about 17 percent—experinces *experiences* hunger on a reguler *regular* basis. You may think this is due to food scarcity, but that isnt the case. In fact, the world produces enough food to feed every one but nutritious food isn't always available. Its mainly a matter of ekanomics: *economics* People cant always afford to eat. And hunger is increasing at a *an* alarming rate, even in the united states. There are many organizations that helps *help* feed hungry people. One of them is the Empty Bowls Project.

Error Summary

Capitalization	2
Language Usage	2
Punctuation:	
Apostrophe	4
Comma	4
Dash	1
Spelling	4

TUESDAY   Week 36

The empty bowls project began in 1990 when a *an* art teacher, john hartom, in detroit, michigan, challenged the students in his High School ceramics class to make 120 bowls for a special occasion. The school district, was hosting an *a* luncheon to raise money for a local food drive. mr. Hartom wanted each geust *guest* to have a unique, artistic bowl for the event. The students met his challenge with success. They made an eye-catching display of their fine bowls and served soup and bread to the staff, who each donated five-dollars to the food drive. Diners were asked to keep their bowls to remind them of the hungry, who's *whose* bowls often are emty. *empty*

Error Summary

Capitalization	10
Language Usage	2
Punctuation:	
Comma	4
Hyphen	2
Period	1
Spelling	3

EDITING KEY:

Name _____

MONDAY   Week 36

Empty Bowls

According to the United Nations' Committee on World Food Security nearly one out of every six people in the world thats about 17 percent—experinces hunger on a reguler basis. You may think this is due to food scarcity but that isnt the case. In fact the world produces enough food to feed every one but nutritious food isn't always available. Its mainly a matter of ekanomics: People cant always afford to eat. And hunger is increasing at a alarming rate, even in the united states. There are many organizations that helps feed hungry people. One of them is the Empty Bowls Project.

- apostrophes
- dashes
- commas
- compound words

TUESDAY   Week 36

The empty bowls project began in 1990 when a art teacher, john hartom, in detroit michigan challenged the students in his High School ceramics class to make 120 bowls for a special occasion. The school district, was hosting an luncheon to raise money for a local food drive. mr Hartom wanted each geust to have a unique artistic bowl for the event. The students met his challenge with success. They made an eye catching display of their fine bowls and served soup and bread to the staff, who each donated five-dollars to the food drive. Diners were asked to keep their bowls to remind them of the hungry, who's bowls often are emty.

WATCH FOR

- names of special projects
- personal names
- place names
- hyphens

WEDNESDAY   Week 36

The food drive at Hartoms school in 1990 was supposed to be a one-time event. However, the handcrafted bowls made quit [quite] an impression. People were deeply moved by the jesture [gesture] of giving the bowls away and a [an] empty bowl became a powerful simble [symbol] of hunger. No one can denies [deny] the symbols potenshul [potential] for making people awarer [more aware] of world hunger. So Hartom with the help of some other people ekspanded [expanded] the idea into the Empty Bowls Project which helps others to host similar events. "Empty Bowls" events take place through out the year all around the united states at least a dozen other countries also participate.

Error Summary

Capitalization	3
Language Usage	3
Punctuation:	
Apostrophe	2
Comma	4
Hyphen	1
Period	1
Spelling	6

THURSDAY   Week 36

One hundred percent of the money collected at "empty bowls" events are [is] given to local national, or international chairitys [charities] that fight hunger. Besides riasing [raising] money, the project also promotes the arts. This is actually one of the projects stated objektifs [objectives]. Participating artists craftspeople and art students donnate [donate] bowls that they make by hand. Bowls are not just [not just] made by ceramics artists but also by artists working with glass wood metal and other materials. Odviously [Obviously], art is a huge part of this project. The founders believe that art helps people finds [find] creative solutions to the worlds problems, including hunger.

Error Summary

Capitalization	2
Language Usage	2
Punctuation:	
Apostrophe	3
Comma	7
Sentence Structure	1
Spelling	5

WEDNESDAY   Week 36

The food drive at Hartoms school in 1990 was supposed to be a one time event. However, the handcrafted bowls made quit an impression. People were deeply moved by the jesture of giving the bowls away and a empty bowl became a powerful simble of hunger. No one can denies the symbols potenshul for making people awarer of world hunger. So Hartom with the help of some other people ekspanded the idea into the Empty Bowls Project which helps others to host similar events. "Empty Bowls" events take place through out the year all around the united states, at least a dozen other countries also participate.

- hyphens
- pronouns
- apostrophes
- words that compare

THURSDAY   Week 36

One hundred percent of the money collected at "empty bowls" events are given to local national, or international chairitys that fight hunger. Besides riasing money, the project also promotes the arts. This is actually one of the projects stated objektifs. Participating artists craftspeople and art students donnate bowls that they make by hand. Bowls are not just made by ceramics artists but also by artists working with glass wood metal and other materials. Odviously, art is a huge part of this project. The founders' believe that art helps people finds creative solutions, to the worlds problems, including hunger.

- verbs
- commas
- apostrophes
- misplaced modifiers

In one or two paragraphs, give your impression of John Carter. Describe his character. Tell what you think he looks like and how he acts. Begin with one of the following sentences, or write your own:

- John Carter of Mars is a swashbuckling adventurer.

- Confident and righteous, John Carter never suffers self-doubt.

Write one or two paragraphs about a superstition that you know about or have read about. If possible, tell about its origins. Begin with one of the following sentences, or write your own:

- Have you ever wondered why it's good luck to find a heads-up penny?

- The superstition that you'll have bad luck if you break a mirror goes back to ancient Roman times.

- There are many superstitions that focus on attracting good luck.

Write a brief persuasive essay that argues the opposite viewpoint to that of "Are Fake Lawns the Answer?" Use one of the following topic sentences, or write your own:

- Fake lawns are not the best alternative to real lawns.

- Although grass needs water and care, nothing can beat the look and feel of a soft, natural lawn.

- Real lawns provide a natural habitat for worms and bugs that are good for the environment.

Write one or two paragraphs for a review of a book or story that you have read recently. State the title and author. Give a brief summary of the plot, the main characters, the setting, and the main ideas. You may want to describe one or two key events, too. Include your opinion of the book or story, but support your statements with meaningful facts from the text, such as carefully chosen quotations. Include information that might prompt readers to seek that book—or to choose a different book instead.

FRIDAY – WEEK 5   **Health Article: The Black Death**

Write one or two paragraphs about the bacterial disease known as the Black Death. Begin with one of the following sentences, or write your own:

- You might think that the plague was wiped out long ago, but you'd be mistaken.

- The Black Death was one of the most devastating pandemics the world has ever known.

- Before antibiotics were developed, bacterial diseases such as the plague could destroy a population.

FRIDAY – WEEK 6   **Mystery: The Mysterious Guest**

Write a new beginning to this mystery without changing the events. You may write your version from the point of view of one of the characters, if you wish. Begin with one of the following sentences, or write your own:

- "This dinner party is going so well," thought Mrs. Singh as she gazed fondly at her guests.

- "I wonder what Mrs. Singh wants," thought the maid as Mrs. Singh summoned her so discreetly.

- Amy was so pleased to be at the Singhs' house for dinner.

FRIDAY – WEEK 7   Problem-Solution Essay: A Slippery Problem

The excessive use of antibacterial soap leads to resistant bacteria. The solution is to use ordinary soap instead. Write a brief problem-solution essay of your own that describes a problem in a convincing way and offers a solution to that problem. Focus on one of the following problems, or choose a different topic:

- Getting plenty of exercise is difficult if you have a busy schedule.

- Keeping your alarm clock close to your bed makes it easy to turn it off and go right back to sleep.

- Having a small apartment is unfair to a large pet, such as a Labrador retriever, that needs space to run around.

FRIDAY – WEEK 8   World Studies Article: The Riace Bronzes

Write one or two paragraphs about the Riace bronzes. Begin with one of the following sentences, or write your own:

- Ancient Greek sculptors made many bronze statues, but few survived to modern times.

- The Riace bronzes are named for the nearby town in Italy where they were found.

- The Riace bronzes are relics of ancient Greek artistry.

FRIDAY – WEEK 9   Character Sketch: Ace Reporter Bly

Write a brief character sketch of a famous person, a character from a book or movie, or someone you know personally. Include details that describe the person's attitudes and actions. Consider using one of the following opening sentences:

- Benjamin Franklin was born poor and died rich, having amassed his wealth through his own effort and hard work.

- Gromit, the faithful dog from the Wallace & Gromit stories, never speaks, but his facial expressions display exactly what is on his mind.

- My best friend's body language always tells me when he's angry.

Write one or two paragraphs about the Lake Michigan Triangle. Begin with one of the following sentences, or write your own:

- The Lake Michigan Triangle may not be as popular as the Bermuda Triangle, but it's just as mysterious.

- Lake Michigan is the setting for frightening tales . . . that are real!

- Strange things happen in the Lake Michigan Triangle.

The Hornbek Homestead is an actual place in Colorado. Write a brief descriptive essay about a place that you have visited or imagined. Use precise and vivid details to create a clear image of the place you are describing. Include sensory details so readers can imagine how the place looks, smells, sounds, and feels. You may want to include figurative language (similes, metaphors, personification, and onomatopoeia) to make the description more interesting.

Write a brief memoir that reflects on one aspect of your life. You could write about a specific event that happened to you, a certain period of your life, an activity that is important to you, or a certain aspect of who you are. Like an autobiography, a memoir is written in first person and tells the truth. By contrast, an autobiography is comprehensive; it tells about your whole life from the time you were born. Use the following opening sentences to inspire your memoir:

- Ever since I was a child, I've been interested in fashion.

- The most difficult goal I ever achieved was running the Chicago Marathon.

- At the family reunion, I met my relatives from Colombia for the first time.

FRIDAY – WEEK 13   **Persuasive Essay: Saving Our Heritage**

Write a brief essay to persuade readers that a particular site, such as the Statue of Liberty or the Great Barrier Reef, deserves to be on the UNESCO World Heritage List. Use your topic sentence to state your opinion. Then give reasons and facts to support your opinion. Remember that a persuasive essay should convince readers to have the same opinion as you do.

FRIDAY – WEEK 14   **Tall Tale: Old Stormalong**

Write one or two paragraphs about Old Stormalong. You can make up a new story about him or retell the same tale in your own words. Include humor and exaggeration, which are two important characteristics of tall tales. Begin with one of the following sentences, or write your own:

- This tale of Old Stormalong and the sea monster will have you on the edge of your seat.

- It wasn't a pretty sight when Stormalong sailed his ship down the waterfall.

- When Stormalong needed a new set of clothes, his tailors certainly had their work cut out for them.

FRIDAY – WEEK 15   **Geography Article: The Legend Behind Spouting Horn**

In one or two paragraphs, describe the geographic landmark known as Spouting Horn. Be sure to tell where it is located and how it was created. You may also want to retell the legend behind this landmark. Begin with one of the following sentences, or write your own:

- Spouting Horn, a natural wonder in Hawaii, has an interesting story behind it.

- According to legend, Spouting Horn began with Liko and the mo'o.

- Like Yellowstone's Old Faithful, Spouting Horn puts on a show for tourists visiting Kauai's south shore.

Write one or two paragraphs about the Tuskegee Airmen. Begin with one of the following sentences, or write your own:

- Although African Americans served in the armed forces before 1941, their career opportunities were limited.

- Named for the place where they trained, the Tuskegee Airmen formed an all-black unit of the military.

- The Tuskegee Airmen paved the way for racial integration in the U.S. military.

"The Grossest Things" tells about two disgusting things that the writer experienced: kissing the Blarney Stone and nearly touching a wall covered with used gum. Write a brief personal narrative about a creepy or unpleasant place that you have visited. Describe the place, as well as your reaction to it. Include as many details as possible so you can communicate your experience to readers. Remember that a personal narrative uses the first-person point of view.

Write one or two paragraphs that give a historical context for the transcontinental railroad. Begin with one of the following sentences, or write your own:

- Establishing the transcontinental railroad was a long process.

- If it hadn't been for the Civil War, the transcontinental railroad may have followed a different route.

- The railroad was once crucial to development in the western United States but is now little more than a memory of the past.

Write a brief descriptive essay about an animal or a scene in nature, such as the migration of stingrays off the coast of Mexico. Use a photograph or nature program for inspiration. Here are some ideas for an opening sentence:

- The water appeared to come alive as the rainbow trout made their way upstream.

- It's hard to see a polar bear against a background of snow.

- A horde of fuzzy brown bats swooped and darted among the trees.

Write one or two paragraphs to describe the activity of bamboo drifting. Begin with one of the following sentences, or write your own:

- Have you ever tried to balance on something really narrow that was floating in water?

- Bamboo drifting is an activity in which a person stands on a bamboo pole that floats in water and uses another pole to help balance.

- Long ago, bamboo drifting was just a means of transportation.

Write one or two paragraphs of a letter in response to the original writer, Samuel, who is in Panama. After writing the date and a salutation, start with one of these sentences, or write your own:

- The family is doing well here in the United States, but we are all worried about your health.

- We have been hearing many scary things about yellow fever in Panama.

- It sounds like the Panama Canal is going to change the world.

Write one or two paragraphs about some of the challenges that Buckminster Fuller wanted to overcome with technology. Begin with one of these sentences, or write your own:

- The construction industry consumes lots of natural resources.

- The open space inside a building is limited by the weight of the materials and the shape of the structure.

- Many construction materials contain toxins.

In one or two paragraphs, retell the news of the historic traffic jam in China. Begin with the date. Be sure to include the most important facts, answering as many of the *who, what, when, where, why,* and *how* questions as possible.

Write one or two paragraphs about diabetes. Begin with one of the following sentences, or write your own:

- There are three types of diabetes.

- Diabetes is on the rise in the United States.

- Maintaining a healthy diet is just one step toward controlling diabetes.

Write one or two paragraphs about the occupation of Alcatraz Island by American Indian activists. Or write a brief article about another social or political movement. Begin with one of the following sentences, or write your own:

- The people who initiated the 1969 movement that took place on Alcatraz Island had a few goals they wanted to accomplish.

- The Boston Tea Party, a movement that took place in 1773, is one of the most famous protests in U.S. history.

- The international Occupy Movement was triggered by events in 2011.

Write one or two blog entries for the Gardeners' Blog. Invent a user name for yourself, and include a posting date. Consider asking a question about plants or giving some advice to other gardeners:

- **Posted by Plantagenet on July 3** Is it true that some roses grow both white and red flowers?

- **Posted by VenusF on August 5** The best carnivorous plants for novice gardeners are pitcher plants.

Write a brief pro-con essay about a specific idea or issue. Be sure to give the arguments for and against that idea and explain why one side of the argument is stronger than the other. Consider one of the following topics, or choose one of your own:

- Some people prefer cats, but I think dogs make better companions.

- Although others may disagree, I believe that school uniforms are a good idea.

- Cellphones may be disruptive in class, but schools should allow students to have them anyway.

FRIDAY – WEEK 28   Sports Article: Games with Flying Discs

Write one or two paragraphs about games that use flying discs. Begin with one of the following sentences, or write your own:

- Ultimate and disc golf have one thing in common: a flying disc.

- Ultimate is a team sport, but disc golf can be played with just one partner.

- If you want a safe sport, try ultimate or disc golf.

FRIDAY – WEEK 29   Science Article: Songs of the Whales

Write one or two paragraphs about whale songs. Begin with one of the following sentences, or write your own:

- The sounds that whales make are surprisingly varied.

- Different types of whales produce different songs.

- Scientists think that whale songs may reveal new information about the world's oceans.

FRIDAY – WEEK 30   Proposal: Peer Mediation Program

Write a proposal for a project or a program that you would like to start at your school. Clearly identify your audience (the person or group that you are writing the proposal to) and your subject. Then write one or two paragraphs to describe the project. Be sure to mention the materials and resources needed to make your proposed project successful. Consider the following topics:

- A class field trip

- An event to raise funds to replace old equipment at the school

- A monthly poetry slam

Write one or two paragraphs to explain how Tamri goats affect the environment in one coastal area of Morocco. Begin with one of the following sentences, or write your own:

- Goats adapt well to their environment.

- Argan trees are highly prized—by people and by Tamri goats.

- Tamri goats love argan berries.

In "Without a Home," the writer reflects on a specific event and tells how he felt about it. Write a brief personal narrative about an experience in your life. Here are some opening sentences for personal narratives that might inspire some ideas:

- I've had to wear braces on my teeth since I was in the sixth grade.

- I share a room with my sister, but we don't agree on how to keep the room clean and tidy.

- For as long as I can remember, the deer that live around here have treated our garden like their own private salad bowl.

Write a short dialogue between two people, one of whom is trying to help the other with a specific issue. Be sure to use quotation marks and identify each speaker. Consider these topics for your dialogue:

- Advising a friend who needs to ask his parents' permission to go on a weekend camping trip

- Advising a friend who is searching for the perfect outfit to wear to a party

- Telling a friend about a good movie worth seeing

Write one or two paragraphs explaining the challenge that animators have in common. Begin with one of the following sentences, or write your own:

- At a certain point, animated figures can become eerily realistic.

- When animated characters are too realistic, viewers' perceptions often fall into the "uncanny valley," from which they regard the characters as creepy.

- People who design video games have to be careful not to make their avatars too realistic.

"A Generous Visitor" is set in the early 1800s. Johnny Appleseed, whose real name was John Chapman, was born in 1774. However, the other characters in the story are fictitious. Write one or two additional paragraphs for the story. Consider one of the following options:

- Tell what happens before Johnny Appleseed knocks at the door.

- Tell what happens when Cora goes to the barn to get her father.

- Tell what happens when Clarence and Martha accept the gifts.

In one or two paragraphs, explain what the Empty Bowls Project is doing to make the world a better place. Begin with one of the following sentences, or write your own:

- The Empty Bowls Project raises funds to feed the hungry.

- Unlike other hunger-fighting programs, Empty Bowls promotes art education.

- The Empty Bowls Project helps people donate in a creative way.

Proofreading Marks

Use these marks to show corrections.

Mark	Meaning	Example
ϑ	Take this out (delete).	I love to to read.
⊙	Add a period.	It was late⊙
≡	Make this a capital letter.	First prize went to maria.
/	Make this a lowercase letter.	We saw a Black Cat.
——	Fix the spelling.	This is our hause.
∧	Add a comma.	Goodnight Mom.
∨	Add an apostrophe.	Its mine.
ʻʻ ʼʼ	Add quotation marks.	Come in he said.
! ?	Add an exclamation point or a question mark.	Help Can you help me
∧̄	Add a hyphen.	Let's go in line skating after school.
∧̄	Add a dash.	That old automobile which is a classic still runs.
‿	Close the space.	Foot ball is fun.
( ) [ ]	Add parentheses or brackets.	My favorite cereals (oatmeal [not instant] and granola) are healthful.
∧	Add a word or phrase.	The red pen is mine.
——	Underline the words.	We read Old Yeller.
∧ ∧	Add a semicolon or a colon.	Alex arrived at 400 Mia arrived later.

Daily Paragraph Editing • EMC 2838 • © Evan-Moor Corp.

Language Handbook

Basic Rules for Writing and Editing

Contents

Capital Letters

Always use a **capital letter** to begin:

the first word of a sentence	Today is the first day of school.
the first word of a quotation, except when it continues the sentence	She said, "Today is the first day of school." **But:** "Today," she said, "is the first day of school."
the salutation (greeting) and the closing in a letter	Dear Grandma, Love, Sherry
the names of days, months, and holidays	The fourth Thursday in November is Thanksgiving.
people's first and last names, their initials, and their titles	Mrs. Cruz and her son Felix met with Principal Bill C. Lee. **Note:** Use abbreviations of titles (for example, Mr., Mrs., Dr., and Capt.) only when you also use the person's name. Did you see the **doctor** yesterday? Yes, I saw **Dr.** Carter.
a word that is used as part of a name or to replace someone's name	I went with **Dad** and **Aunt** Terry to visit **Grandma**. **But:** I went with my **dad** and my **aunt** to visit my **grandma**.
the names of nationalities and languages	Mexican, Cuban, and Nicaraguan people all speak Spanish.
the names of ethnic or cultural groups or geographic identities	There were Asian, Native American, and African dancers at the festival.
the names of ships, planes, and space vehicles	The president flew on <u>Air Force One</u> to see the USS <u>Nimitz</u>, a large U.S. Navy aircraft carrier. **Note:** You must also underline the name of the ship, plane, or space vehicle.
street names	Palm Avenue, Cypress Street, Pine Boulevard
cities, states, countries, and continents	Los Angeles, California, United States of America; Paris, France; Asia, Europe, South America
specific landforms and bodies of water	Great Plains, San Francisco Bay, the Great Lakes
buildings, monuments, and public places	the White House, the Statue of Liberty, Yellowstone National Park
historic events	The Gold Rush began in California. The Civil War ended in 1865.

Daily Paragraph Editing • EMC 2838 • © Evan-Moor Corp.

Capital Letters *(continued)*

each word in the title of a book, story, poem, or magazine (except for a short, unimportant word, such as *a, an, at, for, in,* or *the,* unless it is the first or last word of the title)	The story "The Friendly Fruit Bat" appeared in Ranger Rick magazine and in the science book Flying Mammals.
	
	Note: Underline some titles, but use quotation marks for others:
	    Book titles: Flowers for Algernon
	    Magazine titles: Ranger Rick
	    Movie titles: The Sound of Music
	    TV shows: Sesame Street
	    Newspapers: The Daily News
	But:
	    Story titles: "The Fox and the Crow"
	    Chapter titles: "In Which Piglet Meets a Heffalump"
	    Poem titles: "My Shadow"
	    Song titles: "Battle Hymn of the Republic"
	    Titles of articles: "Ship Sinks in Bay"

Punctuation Marks

Use a **period (.):**

to end a sentence that gives information	The Grand Canyon is in Arizona.
to end a sentence that gives a mild command	Choose a story to read aloud.
with abbreviations (days of the week, months, units of measure, time, etc.)	Jan. (January), Feb. (February), Mon. (Monday), ft. (foot or feet), oz. (ounce or ounces), 8:00 A.M.
with initials	Dr. A. J. Cronin

Use a **question mark (?)** to end a question:

• Did you choose a story to read?

Use an **exclamation point (!)** to end a sentence that expresses strong feelings:

• Wow! That story is really long!

Punctuation *(continued)*

Use a **comma** (**,**) after the salutation (greeting) of a letter and the closing of a letter:

- Dear Uncle Chris **,**

- Yours truly **,**

Use a **comma** (**,**) to separate:

a city and state, or a city and country	El Paso **,** Texas London **,** England **Note:** Also use a comma *after* the state or country in a sentence. Coloma **,** California **,** is where gold was discovered.
the date from the year	October 12 **,** 2004 **Note:** In a sentence, use a comma before and after the year. October 24 **,** 1929 **,** was the start of the Great Depression.
two adjectives that tell about the same noun	Nico is a witty **,** smart boy. **Hint:** Use these two "tests" to see if you need the comma: 1. Switch the order of the adjectives. If the sentence has the same meaning and still makes sense, you must use a comma: Nico is a smart, witty boy. (*This is the same as Nico is a witty, smart boy.*) Nico has dark brown hair. (*It doesn't make sense to say Nico has brown dark hair, so no comma is needed.*) 2. Put the word "and" between the two adjectives. If the sentence still makes sense, you must use a comma: Nico is a witty, smart boy. (*This is the same as Nico is a witty and smart boy.*) Nico has dark brown hair. (*It doesn't make sense to say Nico has dark and brown hair.*)
three or more items in a series	Sarah won't eat beets **,** spinach **,** or shrimp.
the name of the person that someone is addressing and the information that he or she is giving	Sam **,** I think that you should spend less money. I think that you should spend less money **,** Sam. I think **,** Sam **,** that you should spend less money.

Daily Paragraph Editing • EMC 2838 • © Evan-Moor Corp.

Punctuation *(continued)*

Use a **comma** (**,**) to signify a pause:

between a quotation and the rest of the sentence	Mrs. Flores said, "It's time to break the piñata now!" "I know," answered Maya.
after an interjection at the beginning of a sentence	Boy, that's a lot of candy! Oh well, I misjudged.
after a short introductory word or phrase that comes before the main idea of a sentence	Clearly, no one wants dessert. After all that candy, nobody was hungry for cake.
before and after a word or phrase that interrupts the main idea of a sentence	The cake, however, was already on the picnic table.
before and after a phrase that renames or gives more information about the noun that precedes it	Mrs. Lutz, our neighbor, gave Mom the recipe. The cake, which had thick chocolate frosting, melted in the hot sun.
before the conjunction (*and, but, for, nor, or, so, yet*) in a compound sentence	The frosting was melted, but the cake was great. **Note:** A complete sentence includes a <u>subject</u> and a <u>verb</u>, and it expresses a complete thought. A compound sentence joins two simple sentences with a conjunction; each of the two parts of a compound sentence has its own <u>subject</u> and <u>verb</u>. Maya <u>likes</u> the beach, but <u>she</u> <u>prefers</u> the mountains. Maya <u>likes</u> the beach but prefers the mountains.

Use a **semicolon** (**;**) to join two simple sentences that are closely related:

- The party ended at 4:00; the guests left by 4:15.
- The party was great fun; however, the cleanup was exhausting.

Use a **colon** (**:**) to:

introduce a list of items	The café has a few specialties: soup, salad, and dessert.
introduce a sentence, a question, or a quotation	The principal asked an important question: Who will host the book fair while the librarian is on vacation?
show time	The bell rings at 8:20, 12:35, and 3:35 on school days.

Punctuation *(continued)*

Use **quotation marks** (" "):

before and after dialogue (words spoken by someone)	"This was the best birthday party ever!" Maya said. **Note:** A period at the end of a sentence with dialogue always goes inside the quotation marks. A question mark or an exclamation point that follows what the speaker says also goes inside quotation marks. Maya's sister agreed, "Everyone had fun." "May I have a piñata at my birthday party?" Martin asked. Mr. Flores replied, "You bet!" **Be careful!** When the words that tell who is speaking come *before* the quotation, put the comma outside the quotation marks. When the words that tell who is speaking come *after* the quotation, put the comma inside the quotation marks: **Before:** Mrs. Flores asked, "Do you want chocolate cake?" **After:** "I sure do," said Martin.
around a word or phrase being discussed	The word "piñata" is written with a special letter.
around an expression or a word used in an unusual or ironic way	She was "down to the wire" turning in her history essay. Ben thinks the carousel is a "children's" ride.
around the definition of a word	The Latin word <u>geologia</u> means "the study of the earth."

Use an **apostrophe** (') to show possession.

When there is just one owner, add an apostrophe first and then add **s**.	cat + 's ⟶ cat's	The cat's dish was empty.
When there is more than one owner, add **s** first and then add an apostrophe (unless the plural word is irregular, as with the words *children* and *people*).	cat + s' ⟶ cats' **But:**	All of the cats' cages at the shelter were large. The children's cat was in the last cage. Other people's pets were making lots of noise.

Use an **apostrophe** (') when you put two words together to make a contraction.

- I + am ⟶ I'm

- do + not ⟶ don't

Punctuation *(continued)*

Use a **hyphen** (-):

between numbers in a fraction	One-half of the candies have walnuts, and one-quarter have almonds.
to join two words that form an adjective that usually comes before a noun	Beth eats low-fat foods and drinks sugar-free beverages.

Use **parentheses** (**( )**):

to set off a word or words that interrupt, explain, or qualify a main idea in a sentence but that are not essential to the sentence	Many U.S. households (about 40 percent) have dogs as pets. **Note:** If the interruption comes at the end of a sentence, place the end punctuation after the closing parenthesis. If it comes after a phrase that ends with a comma, place the comma after the closing parenthesis. Dogs are popular pets (although cats are also popular). I didn't like the main course (which was grilled tofu), but I ate it anyway.
to set off a nonessential sentence in a paragraph	Dogs are popular pets. (Cats are also popular.) **Note:** The end punctuation goes inside the parentheses.

Use a **dash** (—):

to set off a word or words in a sentence	Many U.S. households—about 40 percent—have dogs as pets. **Note:** There is no letter space before or after the dash.
to show a sudden break or interruption in a sentence	Lexi said I couldn't borrow her skirt—as if I wanted to.

Use **brackets** ([ ]) to set off a word or words that are enclosed by parentheses:

- Jill loved the band (especially the lead singer, Jeff [always dressed in wild, eccentric outfits], who also played guitar) that she saw Saturday night.

Note: Use punctuation with brackets in the same way you would use punctuation with parentheses.

Use **ellipses** (. . .) for a pause or break:

- I couldn't understand the math problem . . . until my friend Angie helped me.

Language Usage

An **adverb** describes action.

Some adjectives can be changed to adverbs with **ly**.	awkward ⟶ awkward + **ly** ⟶ awkwardly quick ⟶ quick + **ly** ⟶ quickly
Some common adverbs do not end in **ly**.	He ran **fast**. We worked **harder** than ever before. The girls sang **high** but the boys sang **low**. The book was **well** worth reading.

Sentence Structure

Writing that has **parallel structure** uses the same pattern of words, phrases, and clauses for a series of items in a sentence. Use parallel structure for a numbered or bulleted list, too.

Not parallel: Ceci wants to snorkle, sail, and to swim during her vacation.	**Parallel:** Ceci wants to snorkle, sail, and swim during her vacation.
Not parallel: Julia told her parents that she plans to get a summer job, that she hopes to earn money for college, and wants to study business.	**Parallel:** Julia told her parents that she plans to get a summer job, that she hopes to earn money for college, and that she wants to study business.

A **modifier** is a word, phrase, or clause that describes another word, phrase, or clause. A modifier that is separated from the word or words that it modifies is called a **misplaced modifier**.

Wrongly placed adverbs such as *only, just,* and *almost* can change the meaning of a sentence. **Hint:** Identify the modifier. Then ask yourself which word in the sentence you want to modify.	I have only a dozen eggs. (In this example, *only* modifies *dozen*.) I only have a dozen eggs. (In this example, *only* modifies *have*.) Only I have a dozen eggs. (In this example, *only* modifies *I*.)
Wrongly placed phrases can be confusing (and even funny).	The children left to play video games **on their bikes**. **Change to:** The children on their bikes left to play video games.

A **dangling modifier** is a phrase or clause that does not logically agree with the word or words that it seems to modify. Note how each sentence has been edited to fix the dangling modifier.

<u>Stashed away in a drawer</u>, he forgot his textbook. (It was the textbook, not the boy, that was in a drawer!)	He forgot his textbook, which was stashed away in a drawer.
<u>To get the job</u>, an application needs to be filled out. (It's a person, not the application, that wants the job!)	To get the job, you need to fill out an application.

Daily Paragraph Editing • EMC 2838 • © Evan-Moor Corp.